GALVESTON DIET COOKBOOK FOR BEGINNERS

Master Hormonal Balance and Weight Loss: 1500 Days of Quick, Easy, and Delicious Recipes with a Comprehensive 45-Day Meal Plan for Menopausal Health

Haley Horton

TABLE OF CONTENTS

1. BEGINNING A NEW PATH

UNDERSTANDING MENOPAUSE AND ITS EFFECTS ON METABOLISM

Menopause is a natural transition in a woman's life, often accompanied by significant hormonal changes that can have a profound impact on metabolism. Understanding these changes and their effects on the body is crucial for navigating this new path with confidence and resilience. Let's delve into what happens during menopause and how it influences our metabolic processes.

The Menopausal Transition

Menopause typically occurs between the ages of 45 and 55, marking the end of a woman's reproductive years. It's officially defined as the cessation of menstrual periods for 12 consecutive months. This transition is primarily driven by the gradual decline in the production of estrogen and progesterone, two key hormones produced by the ovaries. As these hormone levels fluctuate and eventually decrease, women may experience a range of symptoms, including hot flashes, night sweats, mood swings, and changes in weight. Among these, the impact on metabolism can be one of the most challenging aspects to manage.

Hormones and Metabolism

Metabolism is the process by which our bodies convert food into energy. This involves a complex interplay of hormones that regulate how we use and store energy. Estrogen, in particular, plays a significant role in maintaining metabolic function.

When estrogen levels drop during menopause, it can lead to several metabolic changes, including:

- **Reduced Basal Metabolic Rate (BMR):** Basal Metabolic Rate is the number of calories your body needs to maintain basic physiological functions at rest. A decline in estrogen can cause a reduction in BMR, meaning your body burns fewer calories at rest, making it easier to gain weight.
- **Changes in Fat Distribution:** Estrogen helps regulate fat distribution in the body. Lower levels of estrogen can lead to an increase in abdominal fat, often referred to as visceral fat, which is associated with a higher risk of metabolic diseases like type 2 diabetes and cardiovascular disease.
- **Insulin Resistance:** Menopause can also impact how the body handles insulin, the hormone responsible for regulating blood sugar levels. Lower estrogen levels can contribute to insulin resistance, where the body's cells become less responsive to insulin, leading to higher blood sugar levels and an increased risk of developing type 2 diabetes.

Weight Gain and Menopause

One of the most common concerns during menopause is weight gain. While hormonal changes play a significant role, other factors can also contribute to this issue:

- **Age-Related Muscle Loss:** As we age, we naturally lose muscle mass, which can lower our metabolic rate. This makes it easier to gain weight, especially if physical activity levels decrease over time.
- **Lifestyle Factors:** Changes in lifestyle, such as reduced physical activity and poor dietary habits, can exacerbate weight gain during menopause. Additionally, stress and sleep disturbances, common during this life stage, can further impact weight management.

Understanding that weight gain during menopause is influenced by a combination of hormonal changes and lifestyle factors is crucial. It highlights the importance of adopting a holistic approach to managing weight and maintaining overall health.

Strategies for Managing Metabolic Changes

While the metabolic changes during menopause can be challenging, they are not insurmountable. By making informed lifestyle choices, you can manage these changes effectively and improve your overall well-being. Here are some strategies to consider:

1. **Balanced Nutrition:**
    - **Focus on Whole Foods:** Prioritize whole, nutrient-dense foods, such as fruits, vegetables, lean proteins, whole grains, and healthy fats. These foods provide essential nutrients and help regulate blood sugar levels.
    - **Monitor Portion Sizes:** With a lower BMR, it's important to be mindful of portion sizes to avoid overeating. Listen to your body's hunger and fullness cues.
    - **Limit Processed Foods:** Reduce the intake of processed foods high in sugar, unhealthy fats, and refined carbohydrates, which can contribute to weight gain and metabolic issues.

2. **Regular Physical Activity:**
    o **Incorporate Strength Training:** Strength training helps build and maintain muscle mass, which can boost your metabolic rate. Aim for at least two days of strength training exercises per week.
    o **Stay Active:** Engage in regular physical activity, such as walking, swimming, or cycling, to support cardiovascular health and overall fitness.
    o **Flexibility and Balance Exercises:** Incorporate activities like yoga or Pilates to improve flexibility, balance, and overall well-being.
3. **Mindful Eating:**
    o **Practice Mindfulness:** Pay attention to what and how you eat. Mindful eating can help you make healthier food choices and avoid emotional eating.
    o **Stay Hydrated:** Drink plenty of water throughout the day to stay hydrated and support metabolic processes.
4. **Manage Stress:**
    o **Stress Reduction Techniques:** Practice stress reduction techniques such as meditation, deep breathing, or journaling to manage stress levels, which can impact metabolism and weight.
    o **Adequate Sleep:** Ensure you get enough quality sleep each night. Poor sleep can disrupt hormones that regulate hunger and metabolism, contributing to weight gain.
5. **Monitor Health Indicators:**
    o **Regular Check-Ups:** Schedule regular health check-ups to monitor key health indicators, such as blood sugar levels, cholesterol, and blood pressure. Early detection of any issues can help you take proactive steps to manage them.

ESSENTIAL TACTICS FOR HORMONAL BALANCE

The food you eat plays a crucial role in maintaining hormonal balance. By focusing on nutrient-dense, whole foods, you can support your body's natural processes and mitigate some of the common symptoms associated with menopause.

Prioritize Healthy Fats

Healthy fats are vital for hormone production and regulation. Include sources of omega-3 fatty acids, such as fatty fish (like salmon and mackerel), flaxseeds, chia seeds, and walnuts. These fats help reduce inflammation and support brain health, which is particularly important during menopause. Monounsaturated fats, found in avocados, olive oil, and nuts, also contribute to hormonal health. They provide essential building blocks for hormone synthesis and help maintain stable blood sugar levels.

Incorporate Protein-Rich Foods

Protein is essential for maintaining muscle mass and supporting metabolic health. Aim to include a variety of high-quality protein sources in your diet, such as lean meats, poultry, fish, eggs, legumes, and dairy or plant-based alternatives. Protein also plays a role in satiety, helping to manage hunger and maintain a healthy weight, which can be more challenging during menopause due to metabolic changes.

Embrace Phytoestrogens

Phytoestrogens are plant compounds that can mimic the effects of estrogen in the body. They can be particularly beneficial during menopause when natural estrogen levels decline. Foods rich in phytoestrogens include soy products (tofu, tempeh, edamame), flaxseeds, sesame seeds, and legumes. Incorporating these foods into your diet may help alleviate some menopausal symptoms, such as hot flashes and night sweats, by providing a gentle estrogenic effect.

Regular Physical Activity

Exercise is a powerful tool for maintaining hormonal balance. It helps regulate cortisol (the stress hormone), supports metabolic health, and improves mood and energy levels.

Strength Training

Strength training is particularly beneficial during menopause as it helps combat muscle loss, which can slow metabolism and contribute to weight gain. Aim for at least two sessions of strength training per week, focusing on all major muscle groups.

Cardiovascular Exercise

Cardio exercises, such as walking, jogging, cycling, or swimming, help improve cardiovascular health, manage weight, and reduce the risk of chronic diseases. Incorporate at least 150 minutes of moderate-intensity cardio activity each week for optimal benefits.

Flexibility and Balance

Activities like yoga and Pilates enhance flexibility, balance, and overall well-being. These exercises can also reduce stress and improve sleep quality, both of which are crucial for maintaining hormonal balance.

Stress Management

Chronic stress can wreak havoc on your hormones, exacerbating menopausal symptoms. Implementing effective stress management techniques can help keep cortisol levels in check and support overall hormonal health.

Mindfulness and Meditation

Mindfulness practices, such as meditation, deep breathing exercises, and progressive muscle relaxation, can help reduce stress and promote a sense of calm. Regular practice can improve emotional resilience and help manage menopausal symptoms.

Prioritize Sleep

Quality sleep is essential for hormonal regulation. Aim for 7-9 hours of sleep each night and establish a consistent sleep routine. Create a relaxing bedtime environment, limit exposure to screens before bed, and consider natural sleep aids like chamomile tea or magnesium supplements if needed.

Hydration and Detoxification

Staying well-hydrated is important for overall health and can help manage menopausal symptoms like bloating and hot flashes. Aim to drink at least eight glasses of water a day, and consider herbal teas for additional benefits. Supporting your body's natural detoxification processes can also promote hormonal balance. Foods rich in antioxidants, such as berries, leafy greens, and cruciferous vegetables (broccoli, cauliflower, Brussels sprouts), help eliminate toxins and support liver health, which is crucial for hormone metabolism.

Supplementation

While a balanced diet is the foundation of hormonal health, certain supplements can provide additional support during menopause. Always consult with a healthcare provider before starting any new supplement regimen.

Vitamin D

Vitamin D is essential for bone health and immune function. Many women are deficient in this vitamin, especially during menopause. Ensure you get adequate sunlight exposure or consider a vitamin D supplement if needed.

Magnesium

Magnesium supports relaxation, sleep, and muscle function. It can also help alleviate symptoms such as headaches, muscle cramps, and insomnia. Foods rich in magnesium include leafy greens, nuts, seeds, and whole grains.

B Vitamins

B vitamins play a crucial role in energy production and hormone regulation. They can help manage stress and support cognitive function. Include a variety of foods rich in B vitamins, such as whole grains, lean meats, eggs, and legumes, or consider a B-complex supplement.

Hormone Replacement Therapy (HRT)

For some women, hormone replacement therapy (HRT) can be an effective way to manage severe menopausal symptoms. HRT involves supplementing the body with estrogen, progesterone, or a combination of both to balance hormone levels. It's important to discuss the potential risks and benefits of HRT with your healthcare provider to determine if it's the right option for you. There are different types of HRT, including systemic and localized treatments, and your doctor can help you choose the best approach based on your symptoms and health profile.

Herbal Remedies

Several herbal remedies have been traditionally used to support hormonal balance and alleviate menopausal symptoms. While more research is needed, some women find relief with the following herbs:

- **Black Cohosh:** Often used to reduce hot flashes and night sweats.
- **Red Clover:** Contains phytoestrogens that may help with hot flashes and bone health.
- **Dong Quai:** Traditionally used in Chinese medicine to support female hormonal health.

Always consult with a healthcare provider before starting any herbal supplements, as they can interact with medications and may not be suitable for everyone.

DIETARY APPROACHES FOR MENOPAUSAL HEALTH

Whole, nutrient-dense foods should be the cornerstone of your diet. These foods provide essential vitamins, minerals, and antioxidants that support hormonal health and overall well-being. Prioritize a variety of colorful fruits and vegetables, lean proteins, healthy fats, and whole grains.

Fruits and Vegetables

Fruits and vegetables are packed with vitamins, minerals, and antioxidants that can help reduce inflammation and support overall health. Aim to fill half your plate with a diverse range of produce, ensuring you get a mix of different nutrients. Cruciferous vegetables like broccoli, cauliflower, and Brussels sprouts are particularly beneficial due to their hormone-regulating properties.

Lean Proteins

Protein is essential for maintaining muscle mass, which tends to decrease during menopause. Incorporate lean proteins such as chicken, turkey, fish, legumes, and tofu into your meals. Fish, especially fatty fish like salmon and mackerel, provide omega-3 fatty acids, which are crucial for reducing inflammation and supporting brain health.

Healthy Fats

Healthy fats are vital for hormone production and overall health. Include sources of unsaturated fats, such as avocados, nuts, seeds, and olive oil. Omega-3 fatty acids, found in fish, flaxseeds, and walnuts, are particularly important for their anti-inflammatory properties.

Whole Grains

Whole grains like quinoa, brown rice, oats, and whole wheat provide fiber, which helps regulate blood sugar levels and supports digestive health. Fiber is also crucial for maintaining a healthy weight, as it promotes satiety and prevents overeating.

Manage Blood Sugar Levels

Fluctuating blood sugar levels can exacerbate menopausal symptoms such as fatigue, irritability, and weight gain. Stabilizing your blood sugar through diet is essential for maintaining energy levels and overall well-being.

Low Glycemic Index Foods

Choose foods with a low glycemic index (GI) to prevent rapid spikes and drops in blood sugar. Low GI foods include non-starchy vegetables, legumes, whole grains, and most fruits. Avoid high GI foods such as sugary snacks, refined carbohydrates, and processed foods.

Balanced Meals

Ensure your meals are balanced with a combination of protein, healthy fats, and complex carbohydrates. This balance helps slow the absorption of sugar into the bloodstream, providing a steady supply of energy and preventing blood sugar crashes.

Incorporate Phytoestrogens

Phytoestrogens are plant compounds that mimic estrogen in the body and can help alleviate menopausal symptoms. Including phytoestrogen-rich foods in your diet may provide relief from hot flashes and support overall hormonal balance.

Soy Products

Soy products, such as tofu, tempeh, edamame, and soy milk, are rich in isoflavones, a type of phytoestrogen. These foods can be incorporated into various meals, providing a plant-based source of protein and beneficial compounds for hormonal health.

Flaxseeds and Sesame Seeds

Flaxseeds and sesame seeds are excellent sources of lignans, another type of phytoestrogen. Add ground flaxseeds to smoothies, yogurt, or oatmeal, and sprinkle sesame seeds on salads, stir-fries, or baked goods for an added nutritional boost.

Hydration and Detoxification

Proper hydration is crucial for overall health and can help manage menopausal symptoms like bloating and hot flashes. Aim to drink at least eight glasses of water daily and consider incorporating hydrating foods such as cucumbers, watermelon, and leafy greens.

Herbal Teas

Herbal teas can be a soothing and hydrating option. Teas like chamomile, peppermint, and ginger can help with digestion and relaxation. Additionally, some herbal teas may have mild phytoestrogenic effects that can support hormonal balance.

Detoxifying Foods

Include foods that support the body's natural detoxification processes. Cruciferous vegetables, garlic, onions, and citrus fruits are known for their detoxifying properties. These foods support liver function, which is essential for hormone metabolism and overall health.

Mindful Eating

Mindful eating involves paying attention to what and how you eat, fostering a healthier relationship with food. This practice can help you make better food choices, manage portions, and enjoy your meals more fully.

Slow Down

Take your time to eat and savor each bite. Eating slowly can help you recognize your body's hunger and fullness cues, preventing overeating and promoting better digestion.

Listen to Your Body

Tune in to your body's signals and eat when you're hungry, stopping when you're satisfied. Avoid eating out of boredom, stress, or emotional triggers. Instead, find healthy ways to cope with emotions, such as taking a walk, practicing yoga, or journaling.

Supplement Wisely

While a balanced diet is the foundation of good health, certain supplements can provide additional support during menopause. Always consult with a healthcare provider before starting any new supplement regimen to ensure they are appropriate for your individual needs.

Vitamin D and Calcium

Vitamin D and calcium are essential for bone health, which is particularly important during menopause when the risk of osteoporosis increases. Ensure you get adequate sunlight exposure or consider a vitamin D supplement, and include calcium-rich foods like dairy products, leafy greens, and fortified plant-based milks.

Magnesium

Magnesium supports relaxation, sleep, and muscle function. It can help alleviate symptoms such as headaches, muscle cramps, and insomnia. Foods rich in magnesium include leafy greens, nuts, seeds, and whole grains.

Omega-3 Fatty Acids

Omega-3 supplements, such as fish oil or algae oil, can support heart health, reduce inflammation, and improve mood. If you don't consume enough omega-3-rich foods, consider adding a supplement to your regimen.

Personalized Nutrition

Every woman's experience with menopause is unique, and dietary needs can vary. Consider working with a registered dietitian or nutritionist who specializes in menopausal health to create a personalized nutrition plan that meets your specific needs and goals.

INITIAL STEPS: MENTALLY PREPARING FOR NUTRITIONAL CHANGES

Acknowledge the Transition

The first step in mentally preparing for nutritional changes is to acknowledge the transition you are about to undertake. Menopause brings a host of physical and emotional changes that can affect your relationship with food and your body. Recognize that this is a new chapter in your life, one that offers the opportunity to prioritize your health and well-being. Accepting the natural progression of menopause can help you approach dietary changes with a positive and open mindset.

Set Realistic Goals

Setting realistic and achievable goals is crucial for maintaining motivation and staying on track. Instead of aiming for drastic transformations, focus on small, incremental changes that can lead to sustainable improvements over time.

Short-Term Goals

Short-term goals can provide immediate satisfaction and help build momentum. These might include incorporating one additional serving of vegetables into your meals each day, reducing sugar intake, or trying a new healthy recipe each week.

Long-Term Goals

Long-term goals are essential for guiding your overall journey. These could involve achieving a healthy weight, improving energy levels, or reducing the frequency of menopausal symptoms through balanced nutrition. Ensure your goals are specific, measurable, attainable, relevant, and time-bound (SMART) to maintain clarity and focus.

Educate Yourself

Knowledge is empowering. Understanding the science behind nutrition and its impact on menopausal health can strengthen your commitment to making positive changes.

Research and Resources

Take the time to read about menopause and nutrition from reliable sources. Books, reputable websites, and scientific articles can provide valuable insights. Additionally, consider joining support groups or online communities where you can share experiences and learn from others facing similar challenges.

Professional Guidance

Consulting with a nutritionist or dietitian who specializes in menopausal health can offer personalized advice and support. They can help you navigate the complexities of nutritional changes and create a plan tailored to your specific needs.

Cultivate a Positive Mindset

A positive mindset is essential for embracing dietary changes. How you think about food and health can significantly influence your behaviors and outcomes.

Self-Compassion

Be kind to yourself during this transition. Understand that making changes can be challenging, and it's normal to experience setbacks. Practice self-compassion by acknowledging your efforts and celebrating small victories along the way.

Reframe Challenges

Instead of viewing dietary changes as restrictive or burdensome, reframe them as opportunities for growth and self-care. Focus on the positive aspects of nourishing your body with wholesome foods and how these changes can enhance your overall well-being.

Develop Healthy Habits

Creating and maintaining healthy habits can make nutritional changes more manageable and sustainable.

Routine and Consistency

Establishing a routine can help reinforce new behaviors. Plan your meals, set regular eating times, and create a consistent shopping list that includes nutrient-dense foods. Consistency is key to forming lasting habits.

Mindful Eating

Practice mindful eating by paying attention to what and how you eat. Slow down, savor each bite, and listen to your body's hunger and fullness cues. Mindful eating can enhance your enjoyment of food and prevent overeating.

Plan for Success

Preparation is a critical component of successful dietary changes. By planning ahead, you can navigate potential obstacles and stay committed to your goals.

Meal Planning

Take time each week to plan your meals. This can help you make healthier choices, reduce stress, and save time. Consider preparing meals in advance or batch cooking to ensure you always have nutritious options available.

Stock Your Kitchen

Keep your kitchen stocked with healthy staples, such as fruits, vegetables, lean proteins, whole grains, and healthy fats. Having these ingredients readily available can make it easier to prepare balanced meals and avoid unhealthy options.

Build a Support System

Having a support system can provide encouragement and accountability as you navigate dietary changes.

Family and Friends

Share your goals with family and friends and ask for their support. They can help by joining you in healthy eating habits, providing encouragement, and understanding your needs during this transition.

Professional Support

Consider working with a health coach, therapist, or support group to stay motivated and address any emotional challenges that arise. Professional support can offer valuable guidance and help you stay on track.

Monitor Progress and Adjust

Regularly monitoring your progress can help you stay motivated and make necessary adjustments to your plan.

Keep a Journal

Maintain a food journal to track what you eat, how you feel, and any changes in symptoms. This can help you identify patterns and make informed adjustments to your diet.

Celebrate Achievements

Celebrate your successes, no matter how small. Recognizing your progress can boost your confidence and reinforce your commitment to making positive changes.

Stay Flexible

Flexibility is important when making dietary changes. Understand that life is unpredictable, and it's okay to adjust your plan as needed.

Adapt to Changes

Be prepared to adapt your diet based on your body's changing needs and circumstances. Stay open to trying new foods and approaches, and don't be discouraged by setbacks.

2. EXPLORING INTERMITTENT FASTING

BENEFITS OF INTERMITTENT EATING SCHEDULES

One of the primary benefits of intermittent fasting is its positive impact on metabolic health. This eating pattern can help regulate insulin levels, improve insulin sensitivity, and reduce insulin resistance, which is crucial for managing blood sugar levels and preventing type 2 diabetes. During the fasting periods, insulin levels drop, which facilitates fat burning and reduces the risk of insulin-related issues. Moreover, intermittent fasting can increase the production of human growth hormone (HGH), which plays a role in maintaining muscle mass and supporting metabolic function. Higher HGH levels can enhance fat metabolism, improve muscle recovery, and support overall metabolic health.

Weight Management

Weight management is a common concern during menopause, and intermittent fasting can be an effective strategy for achieving and maintaining a healthy weight. By restricting the eating window, you naturally reduce calorie intake, which can lead to weight loss. Additionally, fasting periods encourage the body to use stored fat for energy, promoting fat loss while preserving lean muscle mass.

Intermittent fasting can also help break the cycle of emotional eating and mindless snacking. With a structured eating schedule, you become more mindful of your food choices, leading to healthier eating habits and better portion control.

Improved Digestive Health

Intermittent fasting allows your digestive system to rest and repair, promoting overall digestive health. Extended periods without food can help reduce inflammation in the gut, improve gut microbiome diversity, and alleviate symptoms of digestive disorders such as bloating, gas, and irritable bowel syndrome (IBS). The fasting periods also give your body time to focus on other essential processes, such as cell repair and detoxification, rather than constantly digesting food. This can lead to a more efficient and healthier digestive system.

Enhanced Brain Function

Intermittent fasting has been shown to have several benefits for brain health and cognitive function. Fasting periods stimulate the production of brain-derived neurotrophic factor (BDNF), a protein that supports the growth, development, and survival of neurons. Higher levels of BDNF are associated with improved memory, learning, and overall cognitive function. Furthermore, intermittent fasting can reduce oxidative stress and inflammation, both of which are linked to cognitive decline and neurodegenerative diseases. By promoting a healthier brain environment, intermittent fasting may help protect against conditions such as Alzheimer's disease and dementia.

Hormonal Balance

For women going through menopause, hormonal balance is crucial for managing symptoms and maintaining overall health. Intermittent fasting can help regulate hormones such as insulin, leptin, and ghrelin, which are involved in hunger, satiety, and metabolism. By stabilizing insulin levels, intermittent fasting can prevent the erratic blood sugar spikes and crashes that often lead to mood swings and energy fluctuations. Leptin, the hormone responsible for signaling fullness, can also become more effective, helping you feel satisfied with less food. Ghrelin, known as the hunger hormone, is regulated through fasting, reducing feelings of intense hunger and helping control appetite.

Increased Longevity

Research suggests that intermittent fasting may have longevity benefits. Fasting triggers a process called autophagy, where the body breaks down and removes damaged cells and proteins, promoting cellular repair and regeneration. This process can reduce the risk of chronic diseases, slow down the aging process, and contribute to a longer, healthier life.

Animal studies have shown that intermittent fasting can extend lifespan by improving metabolic function, reducing inflammation, and enhancing resistance to stress. While more research is needed in humans, the existing evidence is promising and suggests potential longevity benefits.

Simplified Eating Patterns

Intermittent fasting simplifies your eating routine by reducing the number of meals you need to plan and prepare each day. This can save time and reduce the stress associated with meal planning, making it easier to stick to healthy eating habits. By focusing on fewer meals, you can prioritize quality over quantity, ensuring that each meal is nutritious and satisfying. This approach can also help reduce the temptation to snack on unhealthy foods, leading to more mindful and deliberate food choices.

Potential for Reduced Inflammation

Chronic inflammation is a common issue during menopause and is linked to various health problems, including cardiovascular disease, arthritis, and cancer. Intermittent fasting has been shown to reduce markers of inflammation, promoting a healthier internal environment. The reduction in inflammation can alleviate menopausal symptoms such as joint pain, hot flashes, and fatigue. By adopting intermittent fasting, you can support your body's natural anti-inflammatory processes and improve overall health.

Flexibility and Adaptability

One of the appealing aspects of intermittent fasting is its flexibility. There are several different fasting schedules to choose from, allowing you to find a routine that fits your lifestyle and preferences. Popular methods include the 16/8 method (16 hours of fasting followed by an 8-hour eating window), the 5:2 method (five days of regular eating and two days of reduced calorie intake), and the eat-stop-eat method (24-hour fasts once or twice a week). This flexibility makes intermittent fasting accessible and sustainable for a wide range of people. You can experiment with different schedules to find what works best for you, adjusting as needed based on your body's response and lifestyle demands.

STARTING GUIDELINES FOR INTERMITTENT FASTING

Intermittent fasting (IF) can be a powerful tool for improving health and managing weight, especially during menopause. However, starting a new eating pattern can feel overwhelming. With the right approach and mindset, you can seamlessly incorporate intermittent fasting into your lifestyle. Here are some guidelines to help you get started on your intermittent fasting journey.

Understand Your Goals

Before embarking on intermittent fasting, it's crucial to understand your personal health goals. Are you aiming to lose weight, improve metabolic health, enhance mental clarity, or reduce inflammation? Clearly defining your objectives will help you choose the most suitable fasting method and stay motivated.

Choose the Right Fasting Method

There are several intermittent fasting methods to choose from, each with its own structure and benefits. Here are a few popular options:

The 16/8 Method

This method involves fasting for 16 hours and eating all your meals within an 8-hour window. For example, you might eat between noon and 8 PM, fasting overnight and into the morning. This approach is straightforward and can fit easily into most daily routines.

The 5:2 Method

With the 5:2 method, you eat normally for five days of the week and restrict your calorie intake to about 500-600 calories on the other two days. This flexibility can make it easier to manage social events and other commitments while still reaping the benefits of intermittent fasting.

The Eat-Stop-Eat Method

This method involves doing a 24-hour fast once or twice a week. For example, you might finish dinner at 7 PM on one day and not eat again until 7 PM the next day. This method can be more challenging but offers significant benefits in terms of calorie restriction and metabolic health.

Ease Into It

Starting intermittent fasting doesn't have to be an abrupt change. Gradually ease into your chosen method to give your body time to adjust. Here's how you can do it:

- **Shorten Your Eating Window:** If you're opting for the 16/8 method, start by reducing your eating window by an hour or two each day until you reach the desired 8-hour window.
- **Reduce Calorie Days:** For the 5:2 method, start with one reduced-calorie day per week before adding the second day.
- **Trial Fasts:** If you're considering the eat-stop-eat method, try a 12 or 16-hour fast first and gradually increase the duration.

Stay Hydrated

Hydration is crucial during fasting periods. Drinking plenty of water can help curb hunger and keep your body functioning optimally. Herbal teas and black coffee are also good options, as they can provide a sense of comfort without breaking your fast. Avoid sugary drinks and sodas, as they can spike insulin levels and negate the benefits of fasting.

Focus on Nutrient-Dense Foods

When you do eat, make sure your meals are packed with nutrients. Prioritize whole, unprocessed foods that provide essential vitamins, minerals, and antioxidants. Here are some tips for creating balanced meals:

- **Protein:** Include lean proteins like chicken, fish, tofu, and legumes to support muscle health and keep you feeling full.
- **Healthy Fats:** Incorporate sources of healthy fats, such as avocados, nuts, seeds, and olive oil, to support hormone production and provide lasting energy.
- **Fiber:** Choose high-fiber foods like vegetables, fruits, whole grains, and legumes to support digestion and maintain steady blood sugar levels.
- **Complex Carbohydrates:** Opt for complex carbs like quinoa, brown rice, and sweet potatoes, which provide sustained energy without causing blood sugar spikes.

Listen to Your Body

Intermittent fasting is not a one-size-fits-all approach. Pay close attention to how your body responds and adjust your plan as needed. Common signs that you may need to tweak your fasting routine include:

- **Fatigue:** If you're feeling excessively tired, you might need to shorten your fasting window or ensure you're eating enough during your eating periods.
- **Irritability:** Feeling irritable can be a sign that your blood sugar levels are too low. Make sure you're consuming balanced meals and consider adjusting your fasting schedule.
- **Difficulty Sleeping:** If fasting is affecting your sleep, try adjusting the timing of your eating window to see if it helps.

Plan for Social Situations

Social situations can be a challenge when you're fasting. It's important to plan ahead and find strategies that allow you to participate without compromising your fasting schedule.

- **Communicate:** Let friends and family know about your fasting plan so they can support you and understand your choices.
- **Flexible Fasting:** Be flexible with your fasting windows. If you have a social event, adjust your eating window to accommodate it, ensuring you stay within your overall fasting schedule.
- **Healthy Choices:** When dining out, choose nutrient-dense options that align with your fasting goals. Most restaurants offer healthy options that can fit into your eating plan.

Monitor Your Progress

Keeping track of your progress can help you stay motivated and make necessary adjustments. Consider using a journal or an app to log your fasting schedule, meals, and how you feel each day. Note any changes in your weight, energy levels, mood, and overall health.

Be Patient and Consistent

Results from intermittent fasting can take time, so it's important to be patient and consistent. Focus on the long-term benefits and remember that intermittent fasting is a lifestyle change, not a quick fix. By sticking to your plan and making adjustments as needed, you'll be more likely to see lasting improvements in your health.

Consult a Healthcare Professional

Before starting intermittent fasting, it's always a good idea to consult with a healthcare professional, especially if you have any underlying health conditions or are taking medication. They can provide personalized advice and ensure that intermittent fasting is safe and appropriate for your situation.

CLARIFYING MYTHS AND REALITIES OF FASTING

Myth 1: Fasting Leads to Muscle Loss

One of the most pervasive myths about intermittent fasting is that it causes muscle loss. The fear is that during fasting periods, the body will break down muscle tissue for energy.

Reality

Intermittent fasting, when done correctly, does not lead to muscle loss. In fact, it can help preserve muscle mass. During fasting, the body first uses glycogen stores for energy and then shifts to burning fat while preserving muscle. Additionally, fasting stimulates the release of human growth hormone (HGH), which helps maintain and even build muscle mass. To further protect muscle, it's crucial to consume adequate protein during eating windows and incorporate strength training exercises into your routine. This combination supports muscle maintenance and growth while benefiting from intermittent fasting.

Myth 2: Fasting Slows Down Metabolism

Another common myth is that intermittent fasting slows down your metabolism, making it harder to lose weight and easier to gain it back.

Reality

Intermittent fasting can actually boost your metabolism. Short-term fasting increases the production of norepinephrine, a hormone that enhances fat burning and boosts metabolic rate. Studies have shown that intermittent fasting can increase metabolic rate by up to 14%. Long-term severe calorie restriction can indeed slow metabolism, but intermittent fasting, when done properly, involves cycling between periods of eating and fasting, which can help maintain a healthy metabolic rate. Eating balanced, nutrient-dense meals during eating windows also supports metabolic health.

Myth 3: Fasting Causes Extreme Hunger

Many people believe that fasting will leave them feeling constantly hungry and deprived, making it unsustainable in the long run.

Reality

While it's normal to feel hungry when you first start intermittent fasting, this sensation often diminishes as your body adapts to the new eating pattern. The body adjusts by improving the regulation of hunger hormones, such as ghrelin and leptin, which helps control appetite and reduce hunger pangs over time. Staying well-hydrated, consuming adequate protein and healthy fats, and eating high-fiber foods during eating windows can help manage hunger and make fasting more comfortable. Additionally, many people report feeling less hungry and more satisfied as their bodies adjust to intermittent fasting.

Myth 4: Fasting is Only for Weight Loss

Intermittent fasting is often associated with weight loss, leading to the misconception that it's only beneficial for those looking to shed pounds.

Reality

While weight loss is a significant benefit of intermittent fasting, it's not the only one. Intermittent fasting has numerous health benefits beyond weight management, including improved insulin sensitivity, reduced inflammation, enhanced brain function, and increased longevity. Fasting can also support heart health by improving cholesterol levels and reducing blood pressure. Its benefits extend to overall metabolic health, making it a valuable approach for anyone looking to enhance their well-being, regardless of weight loss goals.

Myth 5: Fasting is Unsafe for Everyone

Some believe that intermittent fasting is dangerous and unsuitable for most people, especially those with specific health conditions.

Reality

Intermittent fasting is generally safe for most healthy individuals. However, it's not suitable for everyone. People with certain medical conditions, such as diabetes, low blood pressure, or eating disorders, and pregnant or breastfeeding women should avoid fasting or consult a healthcare professional before starting. For those without underlying health issues, intermittent fasting can be a safe and effective way to improve health. It's important to listen to your body and make adjustments as needed, ensuring you approach fasting in a balanced and sustainable way.

Myth 6: Fasting Means Not Eating at All

There's a misconception that fasting requires complete abstinence from all foods and beverages, leading to extreme and potentially harmful practices.

Reality

Intermittent fasting involves cycling between periods of eating and fasting, but it doesn't mean you have to abstain from all food and drink. Most fasting protocols allow the consumption of water, herbal teas, and black coffee during fasting periods.

It's essential to follow a fasting method that fits your lifestyle and dietary needs. Some people may choose to start with shorter fasting periods and gradually increase the duration as they become more comfortable. The key is to find a balance that works for you without resorting to extreme measures.

Myth 7: Fasting Causes Nutrient Deficiencies

A common concern is that intermittent fasting could lead to nutrient deficiencies due to restricted eating windows.

Reality

Intermittent fasting does not inherently cause nutrient deficiencies. The quality of your diet during eating periods is what matters most. By focusing on nutrient-dense, whole foods, you can meet your nutritional needs within the eating windows. Ensure you consume a variety of fruits, vegetables, lean proteins, healthy fats, and whole grains. If you have specific dietary restrictions or concerns, consider consulting with a nutritionist or dietitian to create a meal plan that ensures you're getting all the necessary nutrients.

Myth 8: Fasting is Hard to Maintain

Some people believe that intermittent fasting is too difficult to maintain long-term, making it an impractical approach to healthy eating.

Reality

Intermittent fasting is highly flexible and can be tailored to fit individual preferences and lifestyles. There are various fasting methods, such as the 16/8 method, the 5:2 method, and the eat-stop-eat method, allowing you to choose the one that suits you best.

Many people find that once they adjust to intermittent fasting, it becomes a natural part of their routine. The key is to start slowly, be patient with yourself, and make adjustments as needed. The flexibility of intermittent fasting makes it a sustainable and practical approach for many people.

Embracing the Realities of Fasting

Understanding the realities of intermittent fasting can help you make informed decisions and set realistic expectations. Here's a summary of the key points:

- **Muscle Preservation:** Fasting, combined with adequate protein intake and strength training, helps maintain muscle mass.
- **Metabolic Boost:** Intermittent fasting can increase metabolic rate and support fat burning.
- **Hunger Management:** Initial hunger subsides as your body adjusts, and you can manage it with proper hydration and nutrient-dense foods.
- **Holistic Benefits:** Beyond weight loss, fasting offers numerous health benefits, including improved insulin sensitivity and reduced inflammation.
- **Safety Considerations:** While generally safe for healthy individuals, those with specific health conditions should consult a healthcare professional.
- **Flexible Approach:** Intermittent fasting can be adapted to fit various lifestyles and does not require extreme practices.
- **Nutrient-Rich Diet:** Focus on nutrient-dense foods during eating periods to prevent deficiencies.
- **Sustainability:** With the right approach, intermittent fasting can be a sustainable and practical part of your lifestyle.

ADAPTING FASTING TO EVERYDAY ROUTINES

Before you start intermittent fasting, take a close look at your daily routine. Consider your work schedule, family commitments, social activities, and personal habits. Understanding your lifestyle will help you choose a fasting method that fits naturally into your day.

Work Schedule

If you have a traditional 9-to-5 job, the 16/8 method might be convenient. You can have your first meal around noon, enjoy lunch and dinner, and then begin your fast after your evening meal. If you work night shifts or have a more irregular schedule, you might need to adjust your fasting and eating windows to align with your work hours.

Family Commitments

If you prepare meals for your family, try to synchronize your eating windows with family mealtimes. This approach makes it easier to stick to your fasting schedule without feeling isolated. You might consider eating dinner with your family and then starting your fast until the next day's lunch.

Start Gradually

Jumping straight into a long fasting period can be challenging. Start with shorter fasting windows and gradually increase the duration as your body adapts. For example, you might begin with a 12-hour fast and then extend it to 14 or 16 hours over a few weeks.

Plan Your Meals

Meal planning is essential for maintaining a balanced diet during intermittent fasting. By planning your meals ahead of time, you can ensure that you're consuming nutrient-dense foods that support your health and keep you satisfied.

Balanced Nutrition

Focus on creating balanced meals that include a mix of proteins, healthy fats, complex carbohydrates, and plenty of vegetables. This balance will help you stay full and energized throughout your eating window.

Meal Timing

Consider the timing of your meals within your eating window. Some people prefer to have a larger meal to break their fast and a lighter meal later, while others might split their calories more evenly between two meals. Find what works best for your body and schedule.

Stay Hydrated

Hydration is crucial, especially during fasting periods. Drinking plenty of water helps curb hunger and keeps your body functioning optimally. You can also enjoy herbal teas and black coffee, which can provide comfort and help manage appetite without breaking your fast.

Be Flexible

Flexibility is a vital aspect of making intermittent fasting work with your lifestyle. Life is unpredictable, and there will be days when sticking to your fasting schedule is challenging. Allow yourself the flexibility to adjust your fasting window when necessary without feeling guilty.

Social Events

Social events and special occasions can disrupt your fasting routine. Plan ahead by adjusting your fasting and eating windows on these days. For example, if you have a dinner event, you might start your fast later in the day to accommodate the event.

Travel and Vacations

Travel can also pose challenges to your fasting schedule. Be flexible and adapt your fasting routine to your travel plans. Focus on making healthy food choices and maintaining hydration, and resume your regular fasting schedule when you return.

Listen to Your Body

Your body will give you signals about what it needs. Pay attention to how you feel during fasting and eating periods, and make adjustments based on your energy levels, hunger, and overall well-being.

Hunger Cues

It's normal to feel hungry when you first start intermittent fasting, but this should improve as your body adapts. If you find that you're consistently feeling ravenous or fatigued, you might need to adjust your fasting window or make sure you're eating enough nutrient-dense foods during your eating periods.

Energy Levels

Monitor your energy levels throughout the day. If you notice a dip in energy during your fasting periods, consider incorporating light exercise or a short walk to boost your energy. Conversely, if you feel overly tired or weak, it might be a sign to reassess your fasting schedule or dietary intake.

Incorporate Exercise

Exercise is a crucial component of a healthy lifestyle and can complement your intermittent fasting routine. Plan your workouts around your eating windows to ensure you have enough energy and nutrients to fuel your activity.

Fasting Workouts

Some people find that they can exercise effectively during fasting periods, particularly with light to moderate activities like walking, yoga, or stretching. If you choose to do more intense workouts, you might prefer to schedule them during or immediately after your eating window.

Post-Workout Nutrition

After a workout, focus on replenishing your body with a balanced meal that includes proteins, healthy fats, and complex carbohydrates. This post-workout nutrition supports muscle recovery and energy replenishment.

Manage Stress

Stress can impact your ability to stick to a fasting schedule and affect your overall health. Incorporate stress management techniques into your daily routine to support your intermittent fasting practice.

Mindfulness and Meditation

Practicing mindfulness and meditation can help reduce stress and improve your focus on your health goals. Take a few minutes each day to engage in deep breathing exercises, meditation, or mindful walking.

Quality Sleep

Ensure you're getting enough quality sleep each night. Poor sleep can disrupt hunger hormones and make it more challenging to adhere to your fasting schedule. Establish a regular sleep routine and create a restful sleep environment.

Seek Support

Having a support system can make a significant difference in your intermittent fasting journey. Share your goals with friends, family, or join online communities where you can exchange experiences, tips, and encouragement.

Accountability Partners

Find an accountability partner who is also practicing intermittent fasting. You can motivate each other, share progress, and navigate challenges together.

Reflect and Adjust

Regularly reflect on your intermittent fasting practice and its impact on your health and lifestyle. Be open to making adjustments based on your experiences and changing needs.

Journaling

Keep a journal to track your fasting schedule, meals, energy levels, and how you feel each day. This practice can help you identify patterns, make informed adjustments, and stay motivated.

3. FUNDAMENTALS OF ANTI-INFLAMMATORY DIETS

THE ROLE OF INFLAMMATION IN MENOPAUSE

Menopause is characterized by a significant decline in estrogen levels, which plays a critical role in many bodily functions, including the regulation of the immune response. Estrogen has anti-inflammatory properties, and its reduction during menopause can lead to an increase in inflammatory markers in the body. This heightened inflammatory state can exacerbate menopausal symptoms and contribute to the development of chronic diseases such as cardiovascular disease, osteoporosis, and cognitive decline. By addressing inflammation, you can mitigate some of the negative impacts of menopause and improve your quality of life.

How Inflammation Affects Menopausal Symptoms

Hot Flashes and Night Sweats

One of the most common symptoms of menopause is hot flashes, which are often accompanied by night sweats. Inflammation can influence the body's temperature regulation, making these symptoms more frequent and severe. Reducing inflammation may help alleviate the intensity and frequency of hot flashes and night sweats.

Joint Pain and Muscle Aches

Many women experience joint pain and muscle aches during menopause. Chronic inflammation can exacerbate these symptoms by causing increased wear and tear on the joints and muscles. An anti-inflammatory approach can help reduce pain and improve mobility.

Mood Swings and Depression

Inflammation is also linked to mental health. Increased inflammatory markers can affect neurotransmitter function, leading to mood swings, anxiety, and depression. By managing inflammation, you can support better mental health and emotional stability during menopause.

Weight Gain

Weight gain, particularly around the abdomen, is a common concern during menopause. Inflammation can interfere with insulin sensitivity and metabolic function, making it easier to gain weight. Addressing inflammation through diet and lifestyle changes can help manage weight more effectively.

Anti-Inflammatory Strategies for Menopausal Health

Adopting an anti-inflammatory lifestyle can help mitigate the effects of inflammation and improve menopausal symptoms. Here are some strategies to consider:

Nutrient-Dense Diet

Focus on a diet rich in anti-inflammatory foods that provide essential nutrients and antioxidants. Prioritize fruits, vegetables, lean proteins, healthy fats, and whole grains. These foods can help reduce inflammation and support overall health.

- **Fruits and Vegetables:** These are packed with antioxidants and phytonutrients that combat inflammation. Berries, leafy greens, tomatoes, and cruciferous vegetables like broccoli and cauliflower are particularly beneficial.
- **Healthy Fats:** Omega-3 fatty acids, found in fatty fish, flaxseeds, chia seeds, and walnuts, have potent anti-inflammatory effects. Incorporate these foods into your diet to help reduce inflammation.
- **Whole Grains:** Whole grains such as quinoa, brown rice, and oats provide fiber, which supports gut health and reduces inflammation.

Avoid Pro-Inflammatory Foods

Certain foods can trigger or exacerbate inflammation. Limiting or avoiding these foods can help manage inflammation more effectively.

- **Processed Foods:** Foods high in refined sugars, trans fats, and artificial additives can increase inflammation. Reduce your intake of processed snacks, sugary drinks, and fast food.
- **Red Meat and Processed Meats:** These can contribute to inflammation. Opt for lean proteins like fish, poultry, and plant-based sources instead.
- **Alcohol:** Excessive alcohol consumption can increase inflammation. If you choose to drink, do so in moderation.

Regular Physical Activity

Exercise is a powerful tool for reducing inflammation. Regular physical activity helps regulate the immune system and reduce inflammatory markers in the body.

- **Aerobic Exercise:** Activities like walking, cycling, and swimming can help reduce inflammation and improve cardiovascular health.

- **Strength Training:** Building muscle through strength training exercises can enhance metabolism and support joint health.
- **Flexibility and Balance Exercises:** Incorporate activities like yoga and Pilates to improve flexibility, balance, and overall well-being.

Stress Management

Chronic stress can elevate inflammation levels. Implementing stress management techniques can help lower inflammation and improve your overall health.

- **Mindfulness and Meditation:** Practices like mindfulness meditation and deep breathing exercises can reduce stress and lower inflammatory markers.
- **Adequate Sleep:** Ensure you get enough quality sleep each night. Poor sleep can increase inflammation and worsen menopausal symptoms.

Hydration

Staying well-hydrated is essential for maintaining overall health and reducing inflammation. Drink plenty of water throughout the day and consider herbal teas with anti-inflammatory properties, such as green tea and chamomile.

Supplements and Natural Remedies

Certain supplements and natural remedies can support an anti-inflammatory lifestyle and alleviate menopausal symptoms. Always consult with a healthcare professional before starting any new supplement regimen.

- **Omega-3 Fatty Acids:** Fish oil supplements can help reduce inflammation and support heart and brain health.
- **Turmeric:** Curcumin, the active ingredient in turmeric, has strong anti-inflammatory properties. Consider adding turmeric to your diet or taking a curcumin supplement.
- **Vitamin D:** Adequate vitamin D levels are essential for bone health and immune function. If you're not getting enough sunlight, consider a vitamin D supplement.
- **Probiotics:** A healthy gut microbiome can help reduce inflammation. Probiotic supplements or fermented foods like yogurt, kefir, and sauerkraut can support gut health.

Personalized Approach

Every woman's experience with menopause is unique, and the same goes for managing inflammation. It's important to listen to your body and work with healthcare providers to create a personalized plan that addresses your specific needs and concerns. Regular check-ups with your healthcare provider can help monitor inflammatory markers and adjust your approach as needed. They can also provide guidance on integrating anti-inflammatory strategies into your overall health plan.

ESSENTIAL ANTI-INFLAMMATORY INGREDIENTS

Colorful Fruits and Vegetables

Fruits and vegetables are packed with antioxidants, vitamins, and minerals that help reduce inflammation and support overall health. Aim for a variety of colors to ensure you get a wide range of nutrients.

Berries

Berries like blueberries, strawberries, raspberries, and blackberries are rich in antioxidants called anthocyanins, which have powerful anti-inflammatory effects. They also contain fiber, which supports gut health and helps regulate blood sugar levels.

Leafy Greens

Leafy greens such as spinach, kale, and Swiss chard are excellent sources of vitamins A, C, and K, as well as antioxidants and phytonutrients that reduce inflammation. They also provide magnesium, which can help alleviate muscle cramps and improve mood.

Cruciferous Vegetables

Cruciferous vegetables like broccoli, cauliflower, Brussels sprouts, and cabbage contain sulforaphane, a compound that helps detoxify the body and reduce inflammation. These vegetables are also high in fiber and essential vitamins.

Tomatoes

Tomatoes are rich in lycopene, an antioxidant that has been shown to reduce inflammation, particularly in the lungs and other areas of the body. Cooking tomatoes increases the bioavailability of lycopene, making dishes like tomato sauce or roasted tomatoes excellent choices.

Healthy Fats

Healthy fats are crucial for reducing inflammation and supporting overall health. They help maintain cell structure, provide energy, and support the absorption of fat-soluble vitamins.

Omega-3 Fatty Acids

Omega-3 fatty acids, found in fatty fish such as salmon, mackerel, sardines, and trout, are among the most potent anti-inflammatory nutrients. They help reduce the production of inflammatory molecules and improve heart and brain health.

Avocados

Avocados are rich in monounsaturated fats, which have anti-inflammatory properties. They also contain fiber, potassium, and magnesium, making them a nutrient-dense addition to any diet.

Nuts and Seeds

Nuts and seeds, including almonds, walnuts, flaxseeds, chia seeds, and hemp seeds, provide healthy fats, fiber, and antioxidants. Walnuts, in particular, are a good source of omega-3 fatty acids, while flaxseeds and chia seeds offer plant-based omega-3s and lignans, which have additional anti-inflammatory benefits.

Whole Grains

Whole grains are an excellent source of fiber, vitamins, and minerals. They help regulate blood sugar levels and provide sustained energy, reducing the risk of inflammation.

Quinoa

Quinoa is a gluten-free whole grain that is high in protein, fiber, and various antioxidants. It contains all nine essential amino acids, making it a complete protein source that supports muscle health and overall well-being.

Brown Rice

Brown rice is less processed than white rice, retaining its bran and germ, which are rich in fiber and nutrients. Its complex carbohydrates provide steady energy and support digestive health.

Oats

Oats are a fantastic source of soluble fiber called beta-glucan, which helps reduce cholesterol levels and supports heart health. They also contain antioxidants called avenanthramides that have anti-inflammatory properties.

Spices and Herbs

Spices and herbs not only enhance the flavor of your meals but also provide significant anti-inflammatory benefits.

Turmeric

Turmeric contains curcumin, a powerful anti-inflammatory compound. Adding turmeric to your diet can help reduce inflammation and support joint and digestive health. Combining turmeric with black pepper enhances the absorption of curcumin.

Ginger

Ginger has been used for centuries for its medicinal properties. It contains gingerol, a compound with strong anti-inflammatory and antioxidant effects. Fresh or powdered ginger can be added to teas, smoothies, soups, and stir-fries.

Garlic

Garlic is rich in sulfur compounds, such as allicin, which have anti-inflammatory and immune-boosting properties. Incorporating fresh garlic into your cooking can help reduce inflammation and support overall health.

Cinnamon

Cinnamon contains cinnamaldehyde, an active compound that helps reduce inflammation and regulate blood sugar levels. Adding cinnamon to your diet can enhance the flavor of various dishes while providing health benefits.

Beverages

What you drink can also impact inflammation. Opt for beverages that provide anti-inflammatory benefits.

Green Tea

Green tea is packed with antioxidants, particularly epigallocatechin gallate (EGCG), which has powerful anti-inflammatory effects. Drinking green tea regularly can support overall health and reduce inflammation.

Herbal Teas

Herbal teas such as chamomile, peppermint, and ginger tea offer anti-inflammatory and soothing properties. These teas can help with digestion, reduce stress, and support a restful night's sleep.

Water

Staying well-hydrated is essential for reducing inflammation and supporting overall health. Aim to drink at least eight glasses of water a day to keep your body hydrated and functioning optimally.

Probiotic-Rich Foods

Probiotics are beneficial bacteria that support gut health, which is closely linked to inflammation. Incorporating probiotic-rich foods can help maintain a healthy balance of gut bacteria and reduce inflammation.

Yogurt

Yogurt with live and active cultures is a great source of probiotics. Choose plain, unsweetened yogurt to avoid added sugars, and consider adding fresh fruits and nuts for added nutrients.

Kefir

Kefir is a fermented dairy drink that is rich in probiotics. It has a tangy taste and can be enjoyed on its own or added to smoothies and other recipes.

Fermented Vegetables

Fermented vegetables like sauerkraut, kimchi, and pickles provide beneficial probiotics and are a flavorful addition to meals. These foods can support gut health and reduce inflammation.

Incorporating Anti-Inflammatory Foods into Your Diet

Incorporating these anti-inflammatory ingredients into your diet doesn't have to be complicated. Start by making small changes, such as adding more fruits and vegetables to your meals, choosing whole grains over refined ones, and incorporating healthy fats. Experiment with different spices and herbs to find flavors you enjoy while reaping their health benefits.

Breakfast Ideas

- **Smoothie:** Blend spinach, berries, flaxseeds, and almond milk for a nutrient-packed smoothie.
- **Oatmeal:** Prepare oatmeal with cinnamon, walnuts, and sliced apples for a hearty and anti-inflammatory breakfast.

Lunch and Dinner Ideas

- **Salad:** Create a colorful salad with leafy greens, tomatoes, avocados, and grilled salmon or tofu, topped with a turmeric-ginger dressing.
- **Stir-Fry:** Make a vegetable stir-fry with broccoli, bell peppers, garlic, and ginger, served over quinoa or brown rice.

Snack Ideas

- **Nuts and Seeds:** Enjoy a handful of almonds, walnuts, or chia seed pudding for a satisfying and anti-inflammatory snack.
- **Yogurt Parfait:** Layer plain yogurt with fresh berries and a sprinkle of flaxseeds or chia seeds.

EXCLUDING PRO-INFLAMMATORY FOODS

Pro-inflammatory foods can trigger or exacerbate inflammation in the body. They often contain high levels of refined sugars, unhealthy fats, and artificial additives that can disrupt metabolic processes and immune responses. Regular consumption of these foods can lead to chronic inflammation, increasing the risk of various health issues, including heart disease, diabetes, and arthritis.

Common Pro-Inflammatory Foods to Avoid

Refined Carbohydrates and Sugars

Refined carbohydrates and sugars are major contributors to inflammation. These include:

- **White Bread and Pastries:** These products are made from refined flour, which can cause spikes in blood sugar levels and promote inflammation.
- **Sugary Beverages:** Sodas, sweetened teas, and energy drinks contain high amounts of added sugars, which can lead to increased inflammatory markers.
- **Candy and Sweets:** These are packed with refined sugars and provide little to no nutritional value, exacerbating inflammation.

Trans Fats

Trans fats are artificial fats found in many processed foods. They are known to increase inflammation and the risk of chronic diseases. Avoid:

- **Fried Foods:** Items like french fries, doughnuts, and fried chicken often contain trans fats.
- **Baked Goods:** Many commercially baked products, such as cookies, crackers, and cakes, contain partially hydrogenated oils, a major source of trans fats.
- **Margarines and Shortenings:** These products are commonly used in processed foods and baking.

Processed Meats

Processed meats contain high levels of saturated fats, sodium, and preservatives, which can contribute to inflammation. These include:

- **Sausages and Hot Dogs:** Often contain nitrates and other preservatives that can trigger inflammatory responses.
- **Bacon and Ham:** High in saturated fats and sodium, both of which can increase inflammation.
- **Deli Meats:** Frequently contain added sugars, unhealthy fats, and preservatives.

Red Meat

While not all red meat is harmful, excessive consumption of certain types can promote inflammation. Red meats high in saturated fats, such as:

- **Beef:** Especially cuts like ribeye and T-bone steak.
- **Pork:** High-fat cuts such as pork chops and ribs.

Moderation is key, and choosing leaner cuts can help reduce the inflammatory impact.

Refined Vegetable Oils

Certain vegetable oils are high in omega-6 fatty acids, which can promote inflammation when consumed in excess. These include:

- **Corn Oil**
- **Soybean Oil**
- **Sunflower Oil**

Balancing omega-6 intake with omega-3-rich foods can help mitigate their inflammatory effects.

Alcohol

Excessive alcohol consumption can disrupt the body's inflammatory balance, leading to increased inflammation. While moderate alcohol intake, particularly red wine, may have some health benefits, it's important to limit consumption to:

- **Women:** No more than one drink per day.
- **Men:** No more than two drinks per day.

Strategies for Reducing Pro-Inflammatory Foods

Eliminating or reducing pro-inflammatory foods from your diet requires mindful planning and substitutions. Here are some strategies to help you transition to an anti-inflammatory diet:

Read Labels

Become an avid label reader. Look for hidden sugars, trans fats, and other unhealthy ingredients in packaged foods. Ingredients to watch out for include:

- **Partially Hydrogenated Oils**
- **High-Fructose Corn Syrup**
- **Artificial Sweeteners and Preservatives**

Cook at Home

Preparing meals at home allows you to control the ingredients and cooking methods. Use fresh, whole foods and avoid processed items. Focus on cooking methods that preserve the nutritional value of your food, such as:

- **Grilling**
- **Steaming**
- **Roasting**

Choose Healthy Fats

Replace unhealthy fats with healthier options. Incorporate more:

- **Olive Oil:** Rich in monounsaturated fats and antioxidants.
- **Avocado Oil:** Great for cooking at high temperatures.
- **Nuts and Seeds:** Provide beneficial fats and nutrients.

Opt for Whole Grains

Instead of refined grains, choose whole grains that are rich in fiber and nutrients, such as:

- **Quinoa**
- **Brown Rice**
- **Whole Wheat**

These grains help maintain stable blood sugar levels and reduce inflammation.

Increase Omega-3 Intake

Balance your intake of omega-6 fatty acids with omega-3-rich foods to help reduce inflammation. Include:

- **Fatty Fish:** Salmon, mackerel, and sardines.
- **Flaxseeds and Chia Seeds:** Plant-based sources of omega-3s.
- **Walnuts:** Another excellent source of omega-3 fatty acids.

Limit Processed Foods

Minimize the consumption of processed foods, which often contain unhealthy fats, sugars, and additives. Instead, focus on whole, unprocessed foods that provide essential nutrients without inflammatory ingredients.

Moderation is Key

While it's important to avoid pro-inflammatory foods, it's also crucial to maintain balance and not feel deprived. Enjoying occasional treats in moderation is okay as long as your overall diet is focused on anti-inflammatory, nutrient-dense foods.

Practical Meal Ideas

Incorporating anti-inflammatory foods into your daily diet can be simple and delicious. Here are some meal ideas to inspire you:

Breakfast

- **Smoothie Bowl:** Blend spinach, berries, and a scoop of flaxseeds with almond milk. Top with chia seeds and sliced almonds.
- **Overnight Oats:** Combine oats with almond milk, chia seeds, and fresh fruit. Let it sit overnight and enjoy a quick, nutritious breakfast.

Lunch

- **Quinoa Salad:** Mix cooked quinoa with cherry tomatoes, cucumber, avocado, and a lemon-tahini dressing.
- **Grilled Salmon:** Serve with a side of steamed broccoli and sweet potato wedges.

Dinner

- **Stir-Fried Vegetables:** Sauté a variety of colorful vegetables in olive oil with garlic and ginger. Serve over brown rice or quinoa.
- **Chicken and Avocado Salad:** Grilled chicken breast on a bed of mixed greens, topped with avocado, walnuts, and a light vinaigrette.

Snacks

- **Nuts and Seeds:** A handful of mixed nuts or a chia seed pudding.
- **Veggie Sticks with Hummus:** Sliced bell peppers, carrots, and cucumber with a side of homemade hummus.

PREPARING YOUR KITCHEN FOR ANTI-INFLAMMATORY COOKING

Stocking Your Pantry

A well-stocked pantry is the foundation of any healthy kitchen. Focus on keeping a variety of whole foods and nutrient-dense ingredients that support an anti-inflammatory diet.

Whole Grains

Whole grains are packed with fiber, vitamins, and minerals that help reduce inflammation. Keep these staples in your pantry:

- **Quinoa**
- **Brown Rice**
- **Oats**
- **Barley**
- **Whole Wheat Pasta**

Legumes

Legumes are excellent sources of protein, fiber, and antioxidants. Include a variety of:

- **Lentils**
- **Chickpeas**
- **Black Beans**
- **Kidney Beans**

Nuts and Seeds

Nuts and seeds provide healthy fats, protein, and essential nutrients. Stock up on:

- **Almonds**
- **Walnuts**
- **Flaxseeds**
- **Chia Seeds**
- **Sunflower Seeds**

Healthy Oils

Healthy oils are crucial for anti-inflammatory cooking. Keep these oils on hand:

- **Extra Virgin Olive Oil**
- **Avocado Oil**
- **Coconut Oil** (use sparingly due to its saturated fat content)

Spices and Herbs

Spices and herbs not only add flavor to your meals but also offer potent anti-inflammatory properties. Essential spices include:

- **Turmeric**
- **Ginger**
- **Cinnamon**
- **Garlic Powder**
- **Oregano**
- **Basil**

Organizing Your Refrigerator

Fresh fruits and vegetables should be the cornerstone of your anti-inflammatory diet. Keeping your refrigerator well-organized and stocked with the right produce can make meal preparation easier and more efficient.

Fresh Vegetables

Include a wide range of colorful vegetables to ensure you get a variety of antioxidants and nutrients:

- **Leafy Greens:** Spinach, kale, Swiss chard
- **Cruciferous Vegetables:** Broccoli, cauliflower, Brussels sprouts
- **Root Vegetables:** Carrots, sweet potatoes, beets
- **Alliums:** Onions, garlic, leeks
- **Peppers:** Bell peppers, chili peppers

Fresh Fruits

Fruits are rich in vitamins, minerals, and antioxidants. Keep a variety of:

- **Berries:** Blueberries, strawberries, raspberries
- **Citrus Fruits:** Oranges, lemons, grapefruits
- **Apples and Pears**
- **Stone Fruits:** Peaches, plums, cherries

Lean Proteins

Protein is vital for maintaining muscle mass and overall health. Stock your refrigerator with:

- **Chicken Breast**
- **Turkey**
- **Fish:** Salmon, mackerel, sardines
- **Tofu and Tempeh**

Fermented Foods

Fermented foods are beneficial for gut health, which is closely linked to inflammation. Include:

- **Yogurt with Live Cultures**
- **Kefir**
- **Sauerkraut**
- **Kimchi**

Essential Kitchen Tools

Having the right tools in your kitchen can simplify the process of preparing anti-inflammatory meals. Here are some essentials:

Quality Cookware

Invest in high-quality, non-toxic cookware to ensure your food is prepared safely:

- **Stainless Steel or Cast Iron Pans**
- **Ceramic Non-Stick Pans**
- **Glass or Stainless Steel Baking Dishes**

Cutting Tools

Good knives and cutting boards are crucial for efficient meal preparation:

- **Chef's Knife**
- **Paring Knife**
- **Wooden or Bamboo Cutting Board**

Food Storage

Proper food storage helps maintain the freshness of your ingredients and reduces waste:

- **Glass Storage Containers**
- **Mason Jars**
- **Reusable Silicone Bags**

Meal Preparation Tips

Preparing meals in advance can help you stick to your anti-inflammatory diet even on busy days. Here are some tips to streamline your meal prep:

Batch Cooking

Cook larger quantities of staples like grains, legumes, and roasted vegetables at the beginning of the week. Store them in the refrigerator or freezer to use in various meals.

Pre-Chopping Vegetables

Wash and chop vegetables in advance so they're ready to toss into salads, stir-fries, or soups. Store them in airtight containers in the refrigerator.

Marinate Proteins

Marinate lean proteins like chicken, turkey, or tofu ahead of time. This not only enhances flavor but also makes cooking faster and easier.

Smoothie Packs

Prepare smoothie packs by portioning out fruits, vegetables, and seeds into individual bags. Store them in the freezer for a quick and nutritious breakfast or snack.

4. CORE PRINCIPLES OF THE GALVESTON DIET

TAILORING MACRONUTRIENTS FOR MENOPAUSAL CHANGES

Macronutrients are the primary nutrients required by the body in large amounts to maintain health and energy levels. They include proteins, fats, and carbohydrates, each playing a unique role in the body.

- **Proteins** are essential for building and repairing tissues, producing enzymes and hormones, and supporting immune function.
- **Fats** provide energy, support cell growth, protect organs, and help in the absorption of certain vitamins.
- **Carbohydrates** are the body's main source of energy, particularly for the brain and muscles during exercise.

The Importance of Protein

During menopause, maintaining muscle mass becomes increasingly important due to the natural decline in estrogen, which can lead to muscle loss and a slower metabolism. Increasing protein intake can help counteract these effects.

Benefits of Protein for Menopausal Women

- **Muscle Maintenance and Growth:** Protein supports the preservation and growth of muscle mass, which is crucial for maintaining a healthy metabolism and preventing age-related muscle loss.
- **Satiety and Weight Management:** Protein helps increase satiety, reducing hunger and aiding in weight management, which can be challenging during menopause.
- **Bone Health:** Adequate protein intake is essential for bone health, helping to prevent osteoporosis, a common concern during menopause.

Recommended Protein Sources

Focus on lean and plant-based protein sources to maximize health benefits:

- **Lean Meats:** Chicken, turkey, lean cuts of beef and pork.
- **Fish:** Salmon, mackerel, tuna, and other fatty fish rich in omega-3 fatty acids.
- **Plant-Based Proteins:** Lentils, chickpeas, quinoa, tofu, tempeh, and edamame.
- **Dairy:** Greek yogurt, cottage cheese, and low-fat cheese.
- **Nuts and Seeds:** Almonds, chia seeds, flaxseeds, and pumpkin seeds.

Embracing Healthy Fats

Fats are crucial for hormone production and overall health, particularly during menopause. The key is to choose healthy fats that support heart health and reduce inflammation.

Benefits of Healthy Fats for Menopausal Women

- **Hormone Production:** Fats are vital for the production of hormones, including estrogen, which declines during menopause.
- **Heart Health:** Healthy fats can help manage cholesterol levels and reduce the risk of heart disease, which increases after menopause.
- **Inflammation Reduction:** Omega-3 fatty acids and other healthy fats have anti-inflammatory properties, helping to manage chronic inflammation associated with menopause.

Recommended Healthy Fat Sources

Incorporate a variety of healthy fats into your diet:

- **Omega-3 Fatty Acids:** Found in fatty fish, flaxseeds, chia seeds, and walnuts.
- **Monounsaturated Fats:** Avocados, olive oil, and nuts like almonds and cashews.
- **Polyunsaturated Fats:** Sunflower seeds, safflower oil, and fatty fish.

Managing Carbohydrate Intake

Carbohydrates are essential for energy but managing the type and amount of carbohydrates is important for menopausal women. Focus on complex carbohydrates that provide sustained energy and support overall health.

Benefits of Complex Carbohydrates for Menopausal Women

- **Steady Energy Levels:** Complex carbohydrates provide a slow release of energy, preventing blood sugar spikes and crashes.
- **Digestive Health:** High-fiber carbohydrates support digestive health and can help prevent constipation, a common issue during menopause.
- **Weight Management:** Fiber-rich foods increase satiety, helping to manage weight by reducing overeating.

Recommended Carbohydrate Sources

Choose whole, unprocessed carbohydrates that are high in fiber:

- **Whole Grains:** Brown rice, quinoa, oats, barley, and whole wheat products.
- **Vegetables:** Leafy greens, broccoli, carrots, sweet potatoes, and other non-starchy vegetables.
- **Fruits:** Berries, apples, pears, and citrus fruits, which are rich in fiber and antioxidants.
- **Legumes:** Lentils, chickpeas, black beans, and other beans.

Balancing Macronutrients for Menopausal Health

Balancing the intake of proteins, fats, and carbohydrates is key to addressing the specific needs of menopausal women. Here are some tips for achieving this balance:

Portion Control and Meal Planning

- **Protein:** Aim for about 20-30 grams of protein per meal. This can help maintain muscle mass and support metabolism.
- **Fats:** Include healthy fats in each meal, but be mindful of portion sizes to avoid excessive calorie intake.
- **Carbohydrates:** Fill half your plate with vegetables, one-quarter with whole grains or legumes, and the remaining quarter with protein.

Sample Meal Ideas

To help you visualize how to balance macronutrients, here are some sample meal ideas:

- **Breakfast:** Greek yogurt topped with berries, chia seeds, and a drizzle of honey. Add a side of whole grain toast with avocado.
- **Lunch:** Quinoa salad with mixed greens, cherry tomatoes, cucumbers, grilled chicken, and a lemon-olive oil dressing.
- **Dinner:** Baked salmon with a side of roasted Brussels sprouts and sweet potato wedges.
- **Snacks:** Apple slices with almond butter or a handful of mixed nuts and seeds.

Monitoring and Adjusting Your Diet

Each woman's experience with menopause is unique, so it's important to monitor how your body responds to dietary changes and adjust accordingly. Keep a food journal to track what you eat, how you feel, and any changes in symptoms. This can help you identify patterns and make informed adjustments to your diet.

Consulting a Professional

Consider working with a nutritionist or dietitian who specializes in menopausal health. They can provide personalized guidance and help you create a tailored plan that meets your individual needs.

FOCUSING ON QUALITY PROTEINS AND BENEFICIAL FATS

Proteins are the building blocks of the body, essential for repairing tissues, producing hormones, and supporting immune function. During menopause, maintaining adequate protein intake is particularly important for preserving muscle mass, which tends to decline with age and hormonal changes.

Benefits of Quality Proteins

- **Muscle Maintenance and Growth:** Protein supports the maintenance and growth of muscle tissue, helping to counteract age-related muscle loss.
- **Metabolic Health:** Adequate protein intake can boost metabolism and aid in weight management by promoting satiety and reducing overall calorie intake.
- **Hormone Production:** Proteins are involved in the synthesis of hormones, which is crucial for regulating bodily functions during menopause.

High-Quality Protein Sources

Incorporate a variety of high-quality protein sources to ensure you get all essential amino acids and other vital nutrients:

- **Lean Meats:** Choose chicken, turkey, and lean cuts of beef and pork. These provide high levels of protein with minimal saturated fat.
- **Fish:** Fatty fish like salmon, mackerel, and sardines are not only rich in protein but also high in omega-3 fatty acids, which have anti-inflammatory properties.
- **Plant-Based Proteins:** Include beans, lentils, chickpeas, quinoa, tofu, and tempeh. These are excellent sources of protein and fiber, supporting digestive health and satiety.

- **Dairy and Alternatives:** Greek yogurt, cottage cheese, and other low-fat dairy products are great sources of protein and calcium. For those who are lactose intolerant, consider fortified plant-based alternatives like almond milk or soy yogurt.
- **Eggs:** Eggs are a versatile and complete protein source, providing all essential amino acids.

Incorporating Beneficial Fats

Fats are essential for absorbing fat-soluble vitamins, supporting cell structure, and producing hormones. However, not all fats are created equal. Focusing on beneficial fats can help reduce inflammation and support overall health during menopause.

Benefits of Healthy Fats

- **Hormonal Balance:** Healthy fats are vital for hormone production and regulation, which is crucial during the hormonal changes of menopause.
- **Heart Health:** Beneficial fats, particularly omega-3 fatty acids, support cardiovascular health by reducing inflammation and improving cholesterol levels.
- **Satiety and Weight Management:** Fats help increase satiety, reducing the likelihood of overeating and supporting weight management.

Sources of Beneficial Fats

Prioritize fats that offer health benefits and avoid those that can contribute to inflammation and other health issues:

- **Omega-3 Fatty Acids:** Found in fatty fish (salmon, mackerel, sardines), flaxseeds, chia seeds, and walnuts. Omega-3s have powerful anti-inflammatory effects and support brain health.
- **Monounsaturated Fats:** Avocados, olive oil, and nuts (such as almonds and cashews) are rich in monounsaturated fats, which support heart health and reduce inflammation.
- **Polyunsaturated Fats:** Include sources like sunflower seeds, safflower oil, and fatty fish. These fats provide essential fatty acids that the body cannot produce on its own.
- **Saturated Fats:** While it's important to limit saturated fat intake, some sources like coconut oil and grass-fed butter can be included in moderation.

Practical Tips for Incorporating Proteins and Fats

Here are some practical tips to help you incorporate high-quality proteins and beneficial fats into your daily meals:

Breakfast

- **Protein-Packed Smoothie:** Blend Greek yogurt, a handful of spinach, chia seeds, and a mix of berries for a nutrient-dense smoothie.
- **Avocado Toast with Eggs:** Top whole grain toast with mashed avocado and a poached egg for a balanced breakfast.
- **Oatmeal with Nuts and Seeds:** Prepare oatmeal with almond milk, and top with flaxseeds, chia seeds, and a handful of walnuts.

Lunch

- **Salmon Salad:** Combine mixed greens, cherry tomatoes, cucumbers, and grilled salmon. Drizzle with olive oil and lemon juice.
- **Quinoa and Black Bean Bowl:** Mix cooked quinoa with black beans, avocado, and a variety of colorful vegetables. Add a dollop of Greek yogurt and salsa.
- **Chicken and Avocado Wrap:** Fill a whole grain wrap with grilled chicken, sliced avocado, lettuce, and a light vinaigrette.

Dinner

- **Grilled Fish and Vegetables:** Serve grilled mackerel or salmon with a side of roasted Brussels sprouts and sweet potato wedges.
- **Lentil Stew:** Prepare a hearty stew with lentils, carrots, celery, and spinach. Season with turmeric and cumin for added anti-inflammatory benefits.
- **Tofu Stir-Fry:** Sauté tofu with broccoli, bell peppers, and snap peas in sesame oil. Add a splash of tamari and fresh ginger.

Snacks

- **Nut Butter with Fruit:** Pair apple slices or celery sticks with almond or peanut butter.
- **Greek Yogurt with Berries:** Enjoy a bowl of Greek yogurt topped with fresh berries and a sprinkle of flaxseeds.
- **Trail Mix:** Create your own trail mix with almonds, walnuts, pumpkin seeds, and dried cranberries.

Mindful Eating and Balance

Balancing your intake of proteins and fats is essential for optimizing health during menopause. Pay attention to portion sizes and aim for a balanced distribution of macronutrients in each meal. Here are some additional tips for mindful eating:

- **Listen to Your Body:** Pay attention to hunger and fullness cues to avoid overeating.
- **Enjoy Your Meals:** Take time to savor your food, chew slowly, and appreciate the flavors and textures.
- **Stay Hydrated:** Drink plenty of water throughout the day to support overall health and well-being.

UNDERSTANDING CARBS AND FIBERS

The Role of Carbohydrates

Carbohydrates are one of the body's main sources of energy. They are broken down into glucose, which fuels the brain, muscles, and other essential functions. However, not all carbs are created equal, and understanding the difference between simple and complex carbohydrates is key to making healthier choices.

Simple Carbohydrates

Simple carbohydrates are quickly broken down by the body, leading to rapid spikes in blood sugar levels. These include sugars found in candies, pastries, sodas, and many processed foods. While they provide quick energy, they often lack essential nutrients and can contribute to weight gain and insulin resistance if consumed in excess.

Complex Carbohydrates

Complex carbohydrates are digested more slowly, providing a steady release of energy. They are rich in nutrients and fiber, which helps maintain stable blood sugar levels and supports overall health. Sources of complex carbohydrates include whole grains, legumes, vegetables, and fruits.

The Benefits of Complex Carbohydrates

Incorporating complex carbohydrates into your diet offers numerous health benefits, particularly during menopause:

- **Steady Energy Levels:** Complex carbs provide sustained energy, preventing the blood sugar spikes and crashes associated with simple carbs.
- **Nutrient-Rich:** They are often high in vitamins, minerals, and antioxidants, supporting overall health and well-being.
- **Satiety and Weight Management:** The fiber in complex carbs helps you feel fuller for longer, aiding in weight management.
- **Digestive Health:** Fiber supports a healthy digestive system by promoting regular bowel movements and preventing constipation.

Choosing the Right Carbohydrates

To maximize the benefits of carbohydrates, focus on whole, unprocessed sources that are rich in nutrients and fiber. Here are some examples:

Whole Grains

Whole grains are minimally processed and retain their bran, germ, and endosperm, providing a rich source of fiber, vitamins, and minerals.

- **Quinoa:** A complete protein source that is high in fiber and essential amino acids.
- **Brown Rice:** A versatile grain that provides sustained energy and supports digestive health.
- **Oats:** Rich in soluble fiber, oats help regulate blood sugar levels and support heart health.
- **Whole Wheat:** Products like whole wheat bread and pasta offer more nutrients and fiber compared to their refined counterparts.

Vegetables

Vegetables are an excellent source of complex carbohydrates, vitamins, and minerals. They are low in calories and high in fiber, making them ideal for maintaining a healthy weight and supporting overall health.

- **Leafy Greens:** Spinach, kale, and Swiss chard are nutrient-dense and low in calories.
- **Root Vegetables:** Carrots, sweet potatoes, and beets provide natural sweetness and a wealth of nutrients.
- **Cruciferous Vegetables:** Broccoli, cauliflower, and Brussels sprouts are high in fiber and antioxidants.

Legumes

Legumes are a fantastic source of complex carbohydrates, protein, and fiber. They are versatile and can be incorporated into a variety of dishes.

- **Lentils:** High in protein and fiber, lentils are great for soups, stews, and salads.
- **Chickpeas:** Also known as garbanzo beans, chickpeas are perfect for making hummus or adding to salads.

- **Black Beans:** These are rich in fiber and protein, making them a hearty addition to many meals.

Fruits

Fruits provide natural sugars along with fiber, vitamins, and antioxidants. Choose whole fruits over juices to get the maximum benefit.

- **Berries:** Blueberries, strawberries, and raspberries are low in sugar and high in fiber and antioxidants.
- **Apples and Pears:** These fruits are rich in soluble fiber, which supports heart health and digestive function.
- **Citrus Fruits:** Oranges, grapefruits, and lemons are high in vitamin C and fiber.

Understanding Fiber

Fiber is a type of carbohydrate that the body cannot digest. It plays a critical role in maintaining digestive health, regulating blood sugar levels, and supporting weight management. There are two main types of fiber: soluble and insoluble.

Soluble Fiber

Soluble fiber dissolves in water to form a gel-like substance. It helps lower blood cholesterol and glucose levels. Good sources of soluble fiber include:

- **Oats**
- **Barley**
- **Beans**
- **Fruits like apples, citrus fruits, and berries**

Insoluble Fiber

Insoluble fiber does not dissolve in water. It adds bulk to the stool and helps food pass more quickly through the stomach and intestines. Good sources of insoluble fiber include:

- **Whole Wheat Products**
- **Nuts and Seeds**
- **Vegetables like carrots, celery, and tomatoes**

Benefits of Fiber for Menopausal Women

Increasing fiber intake during menopause can offer several health benefits:

- **Digestive Health:** Fiber promotes regular bowel movements and prevents constipation, which can be a common issue during menopause.
- **Weight Management:** High-fiber foods are more filling, helping to control appetite and prevent overeating.
- **Blood Sugar Control:** Fiber helps slow the absorption of sugar, reducing blood sugar spikes and supporting insulin sensitivity.
- **Heart Health:** Soluble fiber can help lower cholesterol levels, reducing the risk of heart disease.

Tips for Increasing Fiber Intake

Here are some practical tips to help you increase your fiber intake:

- **Start Your Day with Fiber:** Choose high-fiber breakfast options like oatmeal, whole grain toast, or a smoothie with added flaxseeds or chia seeds.
- **Incorporate More Vegetables:** Add vegetables to every meal, whether it's a side salad, roasted veggies, or adding greens to your smoothie.
- **Snack on Fruits and Nuts:** Keep fruits, nuts, and seeds handy for a quick and healthy fiber-rich snack.
- **Choose Whole Grains:** Replace refined grains with whole grains in your meals. Opt for brown rice, whole wheat pasta, and quinoa.
- **Add Legumes to Your Diet:** Incorporate beans, lentils, and chickpeas into soups, stews, salads, and main dishes.

THE IMPORTANCE OF WATER IN THE DIET

Water is the primary component of the human body, making up about 60% of an adult's body weight. It is involved in various critical functions, including:

- **Transporting Nutrients:** Water helps dissolve and carry nutrients to cells throughout the body.
- **Regulating Body Temperature:** Through sweating and respiration, water helps maintain a stable internal temperature.
- **Supporting Digestion:** Adequate hydration ensures smooth digestion and prevents constipation.
- **Detoxification:** Water aids in flushing out toxins through urine and sweat.
- **Joint Lubrication:** Proper hydration keeps joints lubricated and reduces the risk of joint pain.
- **Maintaining Skin Health:** Hydrated skin appears more elastic and youthful.

Hydration and Menopause

During menopause, hormonal fluctuations can lead to various symptoms that can be alleviated with proper hydration. Some of these symptoms include:

- **Hot Flashes and Night Sweats:** Staying hydrated can help manage the intensity of hot flashes and night sweats by regulating body temperature.
- **Dry Skin:** Hormonal changes can cause skin to become dry and less elastic. Drinking enough water helps maintain skin hydration.
- **Mood Swings:** Dehydration can affect mood and cognitive function. Staying hydrated supports mental clarity and emotional balance.
- **Digestive Issues:** Menopausal women often experience constipation. Adequate water intake promotes healthy digestion and regular bowel movements.
- **Weight Management:** Sometimes, thirst is mistaken for hunger. Drinking water can help control appetite and support weight management.

How Much Water Do You Need?

The amount of water each person needs can vary based on factors such as age, weight, activity level, and climate. A general guideline is to aim for at least eight 8-ounce glasses of water a day, commonly referred to as the "8x8" rule. However, individual needs may be higher, particularly during menopause.

Listen to Your Body

- **Thirst:** Thirst is a clear indicator that your body needs more water. However, it's better not to rely solely on thirst, as the sensation may diminish with age.
- **Urine Color:** A practical way to monitor hydration is by observing the color of your urine. Light yellow or clear urine typically indicates good hydration, while dark yellow suggests you need more water.
- **Dry Mouth and Skin:** These can be signs of dehydration and indicate the need to increase water intake.

Tips for Staying Hydrated

Incorporating more water into your daily routine doesn't have to be challenging. Here are some practical tips to help you stay hydrated:

Start Your Day with Water

Begin each day by drinking a glass of water. This helps kickstart your metabolism and rehydrate your body after a night of rest.

Carry a Water Bottle

Keep a reusable water bottle with you throughout the day. Having water readily available makes it easier to sip regularly.

Infuse Your Water

If plain water doesn't appeal to you, try infusing it with fruits, vegetables, or herbs. Lemon, cucumber, mint, and berries can add a refreshing flavor without added sugars or calories.

Set Reminders

Use your phone or a hydration app to set regular reminders to drink water. This can help you develop a consistent hydration habit.

Eat Water-Rich Foods

Incorporate foods with high water content into your diet. These include:

- **Fruits:** Watermelon, strawberries, oranges, and grapes.
- **Vegetables:** Cucumbers, lettuce, celery, and zucchini.

- **Soups and Broths:** These can contribute to your overall fluid intake.

Hydration and Exercise

Staying hydrated is especially important during physical activity. Exercise increases the body's need for water due to increased sweating and respiration. Here are some tips for staying hydrated during workouts:

- **Pre-Hydrate:** Drink water before starting your workout to ensure you begin hydrated.
- **Sip During Exercise:** Take small sips of water throughout your exercise session to replace lost fluids.
- **Rehydrate Post-Workout:** After exercising, drink water to replenish fluids lost through sweat.

The Role of Electrolytes

Electrolytes are minerals such as sodium, potassium, and magnesium that help maintain fluid balance and support nerve and muscle function. During intense exercise or periods of excessive sweating, it's important to replenish electrolytes. This can be done through:

- **Electrolyte Drinks:** Choose low-sugar options or make your own with water, a pinch of salt, and a splash of fruit juice.
- **Electrolyte-Rich Foods:** Include bananas, avocados, and leafy greens in your diet to help maintain electrolyte balance.

Avoiding Dehydration Pitfalls

While increasing water intake is essential, it's also important to be mindful of factors that can contribute to dehydration:

Caffeine and Alcohol

Both caffeine and alcohol are diuretics, which means they increase urine production and can lead to dehydration. If you consume these beverages, be sure to balance them with extra water.

Sugary Drinks

Sugary sodas and fruit juices can contribute to dehydration due to their high sugar content. Opt for water or herbal teas instead.

Making Hydration a Habit

Consistency is key when it comes to staying hydrated. Here are some strategies to make hydration a regular part of your routine:

- **Hydration Schedule:** Create a schedule that includes specific times to drink water, such as before meals, during breaks, and after workouts.
- **Track Your Intake:** Keep a journal or use an app to log your daily water intake. This can help you stay accountable and make adjustments as needed.
- **Pair with Habits:** Associate drinking water with other daily activities. For example, drink a glass of water after brushing your teeth or when you take a break at work.

5. VIBRANT BEGINNINGS: MORNING RECIPES

ENERGIZING SMOOTHIES AND MORNING BOWLS

BERRY SPINACH SMOOTHIE

PREPARATION TIME: 10 min
COOKING TIME: N/A
MODE OF COOKING: Blending
SERVINGS: 2
INGREDIENTS:

- 1 cup unsweetened almond milk
- 1 cup fresh spinach
- 1/2 cup frozen mixed berries
- 1/2 banana
- 1 Tbsp chia seeds
- 1 Tbsp almond butter
- 1/2 cup ice cubes

DIRECTIONS:

1. Add all ingredients to a blender.
2. Blend on high until smooth and creamy.
3. Pour into glasses and serve immediately.

TIPS:

- Add a scoop of protein powder for an extra protein boost.
- Use fresh berries when in season for a sweeter taste.

NUTRITIONAL VALUES: Calories: 180, Fat: 9g, Carbs: 21g, Protein: 5g, Sugar: 9g

AVOCADO KALE SMOOTHIE BOWL

PREPARATION TIME: 15 min
COOKING TIME: N/A
MODE OF COOKING: Blending
SERVINGS: 2
INGREDIENTS:

- 1 ripe avocado
- 1 cup fresh kale leaves, chopped
- 1 banana
- 1 cup unsweetened coconut milk
- 1 Tbsp hemp seeds
- 1 Tbsp honey
- 1/2 cup ice cubes

DIRECTIONS:

1. Place avocado, kale, banana, coconut milk, hemp seeds, honey, and ice cubes in a blender.
2. Blend until smooth and thick.
3. Pour into bowls and top with additional hemp seeds, sliced banana, and a drizzle of honey.

TIPS:

- Add a handful of spinach for extra nutrients.
- Top with granola for added crunch.

NUTRITIONAL VALUES: Calories: 250, Fat: 17g, Carbs: 27g, Protein: 4g, Sugar: 11g

PEANUT BUTTER BANANA SMOOTHIE

PREPARATION TIME: 5 min
COOKING TIME: N/A
MODE OF COOKING: Blending
SERVINGS: 2
INGREDIENTS:

- 1 cup unsweetened almond milk
- 1 banana
- 2 Tbsp natural peanut butter
- 1 Tbsp flaxseed meal
- 1 tsp vanilla extract
- 1/2 cup ice cubes

DIRECTIONS:

1. Combine all ingredients in a blender.
2. Blend until smooth and creamy.
3. Serve immediately in glasses.

TIPS:

- Add a scoop of chocolate protein powder for a chocolatey twist.
- Use frozen banana slices to make the smoothie thicker.

NUTRITIONAL VALUES: Calories: 210, Fat: 12g, Carbs: 24g, Protein: 6g, Sugar: 12g

TROPICAL GREEN SMOOTHIE BOWL

PREPARATION TIME: 10 min
COOKING TIME: N/A
MODE OF COOKING: Blending
SERVINGS: 2
INGREDIENTS:

- 1 cup unsweetened coconut milk
- 1 cup fresh spinach
- 1/2 cup frozen pineapple chunks
- 1/2 frozen mango chunks
- 1 Tbsp chia seeds
- 1 Tbsp honey
- 1/2 cup ice cubes

DIRECTIONS:

1. Place all ingredients into a blender.
2. Blend on high until smooth.
3. Pour into bowls and top with fresh pineapple slices, shredded coconut, and a sprinkle of chia seeds.

TIPS:

- Add a squeeze of lime juice for a refreshing twist.
- Use fresh mango and pineapple if available.

NUTRITIONAL VALUES: Calories: 190, Fat: 7g, Carbs: 29g, Protein: 3g, Sugar: 21g

CHOCOLATE AVOCADO SMOOTHIE

PREPARATION TIME: 5 min
COOKING TIME: N/A
MODE OF COOKING: Blending
SERVINGS: 2
INGREDIENTS:

- 1 ripe avocado
- 1 banana
- 1 cup unsweetened almond milk
- 2 Tbsp cocoa powder
- 1 Tbsp honey
- 1/2 tsp vanilla extract
- 1/2 cup ice cubes

DIRECTIONS:

1. Combine avocado, banana, almond milk, cocoa powder, honey, vanilla extract, and ice cubes in a blender.
2. Blend until smooth and creamy.
3. Serve immediately.

TIPS:

- Use frozen banana for a thicker texture.
- Add a pinch of cinnamon for extra flavor.

NUTRITIONAL VALUES: Calories: 220, Fat: 14g, Carbs: 28g, Protein: 3g, Sugar: 14g

BERRY PROTEIN SMOOTHIE

PREPARATION TIME: 5 min
COOKING TIME: N/A
MODE OF COOKING: Blending
SERVINGS: 2
INGREDIENTS:

- 1 cup unsweetened almond milk
- 1 cup frozen mixed berries
- 1 banana
- 1 scoop vanilla protein powder
- 1 Tbsp chia seeds
- 1/2 cup ice cubes

DIRECTIONS:

1. Add all ingredients to a blender.
2. Blend until smooth and creamy.
3. Pour into glasses and enjoy immediately.

TIPS:

- Use a mixed berry blend for a variety of flavors.
- Add spinach for extra nutrients without altering the taste.

NUTRITIONAL VALUES: Calories: 190, Fat: 5g, Carbs: 26g, Protein: 15g, Sugar: 14g

PROTEIN-ENRICHED BREAKFAST OPTIONS

GREEK YOGURT PARFAIT

PREPARATION TIME: 10 min
COOKING TIME: N/A
MODE OF COOKING: Assembling
SERVINGS: 2
INGREDIENTS:

- 2 cups Greek yogurt (plain, non-fat)
- 1/2 cup fresh berries (blueberries, strawberries, raspberries)
- 2 Tbsp chia seeds
- 2 Tbsp chopped almonds
- 1 Tbsp honey
- 1/2 tsp vanilla extract

DIRECTIONS:

1. In a bowl, mix Greek yogurt with honey and vanilla extract.
2. Layer yogurt, berries, chia seeds, and almonds in two glasses or bowls.
3. Repeat layers and top with remaining berries and nuts.
4. Serve immediately.

TIPS:

- Use a variety of berries for a more colorful parfait.
- Add a sprinkle of cinnamon for extra flavor.

NUTRITIONAL VALUES: Calories: 200, Fat: 7g, Carbs: 19g, Protein: 15g, Sugar: 12g

SPINACH AND FETA OMELETTE

PREPARATION TIME: 5 min
COOKING TIME: 10 min
MODE OF COOKING: Stovetop
SERVINGS: 2
INGREDIENTS:

- 4 large eggs
- 1/4 cup crumbled feta cheese
- 1 cup fresh spinach, chopped
- 1 Tbsp olive oil
- Salt and pepper to taste

DIRECTIONS:

1. In a bowl, whisk eggs with salt and pepper.
2. Heat olive oil in a non-stick skillet over medium heat.
3. Add spinach and cook until wilted.
4. Pour eggs into the skillet, sprinkle feta on top, and cook until set.
5. Fold the omelette in half and serve immediately.

TIPS:

- Add a handful of cherry tomatoes for extra flavor.
- Serve with a side of avocado slices.

NUTRITIONAL VALUES: Calories: 220, Fat: 18g, Carbs: 3g, Protein: 14g, Sugar: 1g

COTTAGE CHEESE WITH NUTS AND SEEDS

PREPARATION TIME: 5 min
COOKING TIME: N/A
MODE OF COOKING: Assembling
SERVINGS: 2
INGREDIENTS:

- 2 cups low-fat cottage cheese
- 2 Tbsp chopped walnuts
- 1 Tbsp flaxseeds
- 1 Tbsp chia seeds
- 1/4 cup fresh blueberries

DIRECTIONS:

1. Divide cottage cheese between two bowls.
2. Top with chopped walnuts, flaxseeds, chia seeds, and blueberries.
3. Serve immediately.

TIPS:

- Use mixed berries for a variety of flavors.
- Add a drizzle of honey for extra sweetness.

NUTRITIONAL VALUES: Calories: 180, Fat: 8g, Carbs: 12g, Protein: 16g, Sugar: 5g

SMOKED SALMON AND AVOCADO TOAST

PREPARATION TIME: 10 min
COOKING TIME: 5 min
MODE OF COOKING: Stovetop/Toasting
SERVINGS: 2

INGREDIENTS:

- 2 slices whole grain bread
- 1 ripe avocado
- 4 oz smoked salmon
- 1 Tbsp lemon juice

- 1/2 tsp red pepper flakes
- Salt and pepper to taste

DIRECTIONS:

1. Toast the bread slices to your preference.
2. In a bowl, mash the avocado with lemon juice, red pepper flakes, salt, and pepper.
3. Spread the avocado mixture evenly on the toasted bread.
4. Top each slice with smoked salmon.
5. Serve immediately.

TIPS:

- Garnish with fresh dill or chives for added flavor.
- Serve with a side of mixed greens for a complete meal.

NUTRITIONAL VALUES: Calories: 250, Fat: 18g, Carbs: 18g, Protein: 12g, Sugar: 2g

TURKEY AND SPINACH BREAKFAST SKILLET

PREPARATION TIME: 10 min
COOKING TIME: 15 min
MODE OF COOKING: Stovetop
SERVINGS: 2
INGREDIENTS:

- 8 oz ground turkey
- 2 cups fresh spinach, chopped
- 1 small onion, diced
- 1 red bell pepper, diced
- 2 Tbsp olive oil
- 1/2 tsp garlic powder
- Salt and pepper to taste

DIRECTIONS:

1. Heat olive oil in a large skillet over medium heat.
2. Add onion and bell pepper, sauté until soft.
3. Add ground turkey, cook until browned.
4. Stir in spinach, garlic powder, salt, and pepper. Cook until spinach is wilted.
5. Serve hot.

TIPS:

- Add a poached egg on top for extra protein.
- Use ground chicken or beef as a variation.

NUTRITIONAL VALUES: Calories: 300, Fat: 18g, Carbs: 10g, Protein: 25g, Sugar: 4g

PROTEIN PANCAKES

PREPARATION TIME: 10 min
COOKING TIME: 10 min
MODE OF COOKING: Stovetop
SERVINGS: 2
INGREDIENTS:

- 1 cup rolled oats
- 1 ripe banana
- 2 large eggs
- 1/2 cup cottage cheese
- 1 tsp vanilla extract
- 1/2 tsp baking powder
- 1 Tbsp coconut oil (for cooking)

DIRECTIONS:

1. Blend oats in a blender until they become a fine flour.
2. Add banana, eggs, cottage cheese, vanilla extract, and baking powder. Blend until smooth.
3. Heat coconut oil in a non-stick skillet over medium heat.
4. Pour batter into the skillet to form small pancakes.
5. Cook until bubbles form on the surface, then flip and cook until golden brown.
6. Serve hot with fresh berries or a drizzle of honey.

TIPS:

- Add a scoop of protein powder for extra protein.
- Use Greek yogurt instead of cottage cheese for a different texture.

NUTRITIONAL VALUES: Calories: 220, Fat: 10g, Carbs: 22g, Protein: 12g, Sugar: 7g

WARM AND FULFILLING PORRIDGE VARIETIES

CINNAMON APPLE QUINOA PORRIDGE

PREPARATION TIME: 10 min
COOKING TIME: 20 min
MODE OF COOKING: Stovetop
SERVINGS: 2
INGREDIENTS:

- 1 cup quinoa, rinsed
- 2 cups unsweetened almond milk
- 1 apple, diced
- 1 tsp cinnamon
- 1/2 tsp vanilla extract
- 1 Tbsp chia seeds
- 1 Tbsp maple syrup (optional)
- Pinch of salt

DIRECTIONS:

1. In a medium saucepan, combine quinoa, almond milk, apple, cinnamon, vanilla extract, chia seeds, and a pinch of salt.
2. Bring to a boil over medium-high heat, then reduce to a simmer.
3. Cook for 15-20 minutes, stirring occasionally, until the quinoa is tender and the porridge has thickened.
4. Serve hot, drizzled with maple syrup if desired.

TIPS:

- Add a handful of chopped nuts for extra crunch.
- Top with a dollop of Greek yogurt for added protein.

NUTRITIONAL VALUES: Calories: 290, Fat: 7g, Carbs: 45g, Protein: 9g, Sugar: 9g

COCONUT CHIA SEED PORRIDGE

PREPARATION TIME: 5 min
COOKING TIME: 10 min
MODE OF COOKING: Stovetop
SERVINGS: 2
INGREDIENTS:

- 1/2 cup chia seeds
- 2 cups unsweetened coconut milk
- 1/2 tsp vanilla extract
- 1 Tbsp shredded coconut
- 1 Tbsp honey
- Fresh berries for topping

DIRECTIONS:

1. In a medium saucepan, combine chia seeds, coconut milk, and vanilla extract.
2. Bring to a simmer over medium heat, stirring frequently.
3. Cook for 8-10 minutes until the mixture thickens.
4. Divide the porridge into bowls and top with shredded coconut, honey, and fresh berries.

TIPS:

- Soak chia seeds in coconut milk overnight for a quicker breakfast.
- Add a pinch of cinnamon for extra flavor.

NUTRITIONAL VALUES: Calories: 240, Fat: 14g, Carbs: 26g, Protein: 5g, Sugar: 12g

ALMOND BUTTER AND BERRY OATMEAL

PREPARATION TIME: 5 min
COOKING TIME: 10 min
MODE OF COOKING: Stovetop
SERVINGS: 2
INGREDIENTS:

- 1 cup rolled oats
- 2 cups unsweetened almond milk
- 1 Tbsp almond butter
- 1/2 cup fresh or frozen berries
- 1 Tbsp flaxseeds
- 1 Tbsp honey
- Pinch of salt

DIRECTIONS:

1. In a medium saucepan, combine rolled oats, almond milk, and a pinch of salt.
2. Bring to a boil, then reduce heat and simmer for 5-7 minutes, stirring occasionally.
3. Stir in almond butter, berries, and flaxseeds. Cook for an additional 2-3 minutes.
4. Divide into bowls and drizzle with honey.

TIPS:

- Use mixed berries for a variety of flavors.
- Top with sliced bananas for extra sweetness.

NUTRITIONAL VALUES: Calories: 310, Fat: 12g, Carbs: 45g, Protein: 10g, Sugar: 14g

FLAXSEED AND BLUEBERRY AMARANTH PORRIDGE

PREPARATION TIME: 5 min
COOKING TIME: 25 min
MODE OF COOKING: Stovetop
SERVINGS: 2
INGREDIENTS:
- 1 cup amaranth
- 2 1/2 cups water
- 1/2 cup unsweetened almond milk
- 1/2 cup fresh blueberries
- 1 Tbsp flaxseeds
- 1 Tbsp honey
- 1/2 tsp cinnamon
- Pinch of salt

DIRECTIONS:
1. In a medium saucepan, combine amaranth and water. Bring to a boil.
2. Reduce heat to low and simmer for 20-25 minutes, stirring occasionally, until amaranth is tender.
3. Stir in almond milk, blueberries, flaxseeds, honey, cinnamon, and a pinch of salt.
4. Cook for an additional 2-3 minutes until the porridge is heated through.
5. Serve hot.

TIPS:
- Use frozen blueberries if fresh are not available.
- Add a handful of chopped nuts for extra crunch.

NUTRITIONAL VALUES: Calories: 270, Fat: 7g, Carbs: 45g, Protein: 9g, Sugar: 11g

PUMPKIN SPICE QUINOA PORRIDGE

PREPARATION TIME: 10 min
COOKING TIME: 20 min
MODE OF COOKING: Stovetop
SERVINGS: 2
INGREDIENTS:
- 1 cup quinoa, rinsed
- 2 cups unsweetened almond milk
- 1/2 cup pumpkin puree
- 1 tsp pumpkin pie spice
- 1/2 tsp vanilla extract
- 1 Tbsp maple syrup
- 1/4 cup chopped pecans

DIRECTIONS:
1. In a medium saucepan, combine quinoa, almond milk, pumpkin puree, pumpkin pie spice, and vanilla extract.
2. Bring to a boil over medium-high heat, then reduce to a simmer.
3. Cook for 15-20 minutes, stirring occasionally, until quinoa is tender and the porridge has thickened.
4. Stir in maple syrup and divide into bowls.
5. Top with chopped pecans and serve.

TIPS:
- Use canned pumpkin for convenience.
- Add a dollop of Greek yogurt for extra creaminess.

NUTRITIONAL VALUES: Calories: 310, Fat: 10g, Carbs: 45g, Protein: 10g, Sugar: 13g

VANILLA ALMOND PROTEIN PORRIDGE

PREPARATION TIME: 5 min
COOKING TIME: 10 min
MODE OF COOKING: Stovetop
SERVINGS: 2
INGREDIENTS:
- 1 cup rolled oats
- 2 cups unsweetened almond milk
- 1 scoop vanilla protein powder
- 1 Tbsp almond butter
- 1 Tbsp chia seeds
- 1/4 cup sliced almonds
- 1 Tbsp honey

DIRECTIONS:
1. In a medium saucepan, combine rolled oats and almond milk. Bring to a boil.
2. Reduce heat and simmer for 5-7 minutes, stirring occasionally.
3. Stir in protein powder, almond butter, and chia seeds. Cook for an additional 2-3 minutes.
4. Divide into bowls and top with sliced almonds and honey.

TIPS:
- Add fresh or dried fruit for extra sweetness.

NUTRITIONAL VALUES: Calories: 330, Fat: 14g, Carbs: 37g, Protein: 18g, Sugar: 13g

6. LIGHT AND NUTRITIOUS MEALS: SALADS AND VEGGIES

INNOVATIVE AND TASTY SALADS

MEDITERRANEAN CHICKPEA SALAD

PREPARATION TIME: 15 min
COOKING TIME: N/A
MODE OF COOKING: Assembling
SERVINGS: 4
INGREDIENTS:

- 1 can chickpeas, drained and rinsed
- 1 cup cherry tomatoes, halved
- 1 cucumber, diced
- 1/4 cup red onion, finely chopped
- 1/4 cup Kalamata olives, sliced
- 1/4 cup feta cheese, crumbled
- 2 Tbsp fresh parsley, chopped
- 2 Tbsp olive oil
- 1 Tbsp red wine vinegar
- 1 tsp dried oregano
- Salt and pepper to taste

DIRECTIONS:

1. In a large bowl, combine chickpeas, cherry tomatoes, cucumber, red onion, olives, feta cheese, and parsley.
2. In a small bowl, whisk together olive oil, red wine vinegar, oregano, salt, and pepper.
3. Pour the dressing over the salad and toss to combine.
4. Serve immediately or refrigerate until ready to serve.

TIPS:

- Add grilled chicken or shrimp for extra protein.
- Use fresh mint for a different flavor twist.

NUTRITIONAL VALUES: Calories: 220, Fat: 12g, Carbs: 24g, Protein: 7g, Sugar: 4g

SPINACH AND STRAWBERRY SALAD WITH POPPY SEED DRESSING

PREPARATION TIME: 10 min
COOKING TIME: N/A
MODE OF COOKING: Assembling
SERVINGS: 4
INGREDIENTS:

- 6 cups fresh spinach
- 1 cup strawberries, sliced
- 1/4 cup red onion, thinly sliced
- 1/4 cup pecans, toasted
- 1/4 cup feta cheese, crumbled

Dressing:

- 1/4 cup olive oil
- 2 Tbsp apple cider vinegar
- 1 Tbsp honey
- 1 tsp poppy seeds
- Salt and pepper to taste

DIRECTIONS:

1. In a large bowl, combine spinach, strawberries, red onion, pecans, and feta cheese.
2. In a small bowl, whisk together olive oil, apple cider vinegar, honey, poppy seeds, salt, and pepper.
3. Pour the dressing over the salad and toss to combine.
4. Serve immediately.

TIPS:

- Add grilled chicken for a heartier meal.
- Use walnuts or almonds instead of pecans for variety.

NUTRITIONAL VALUES: Calories: 210, Fat: 16g, Carbs: 14g, Protein: 4g, Sugar: 10g

GRILLED CHICKEN AND AVOCADO SALAD

PREPARATION TIME: 15 min
COOKING TIME: 15 min
MODE OF COOKING: Grilling
SERVINGS: 4
INGREDIENTS:

- 2 boneless, skinless chicken breasts
- 1 Tbsp olive oil
- Salt and pepper to taste
- 6 cups mixed greens
- 1 avocado, sliced
- 1/2 cup cherry tomatoes, halved
- 1/4 cup red onion, thinly sliced
- 1/4 cup feta cheese, crumbled

Dressing:

- 1/4 cup olive oil
- 2 Tbsp balsamic vinegar
- 1 tsp Dijon mustard
- 1 tsp honey
- Salt and pepper to taste

DIRECTIONS:

1. Preheat grill to medium-high heat.
2. Brush chicken breasts with olive oil and season with salt and pepper.
3. Grill chicken for 6-7 minutes on each side or until fully cooked.
4. Let chicken rest for 5 minutes, then slice.
5. In a large bowl, combine mixed greens, avocado, cherry tomatoes, red onion, and feta cheese.
6. In a small bowl, whisk together olive oil, balsamic vinegar, Dijon mustard, honey, salt, and pepper.
7. Pour the dressing over the salad and toss to combine.
8. Top with grilled chicken slices and serve immediately.

TIPS:

- Marinate the chicken in lemon juice and herbs for extra flavor.
- Add a hard-boiled egg for additional protein.

NUTRITIONAL VALUES: Calories: 350, Fat: 25g, Carbs: 12g, Protein: 22g, Sugar: 6g

KALE AND QUINOA SALAD WITH LEMON VINAIGRETTE

PREPARATION TIME: 15 min
COOKING TIME: 15 min
MODE OF COOKING: Stovetop
SERVINGS: 4
INGREDIENTS:

- 1 cup quinoa, rinsed
- 2 cups water
- 4 cups kale, chopped
- 1/2 cup shredded carrots
- 1/4 cup dried cranberries
- 1/4 cup sunflower seeds
- 1/4 cup feta cheese, crumbled

Dressing:

- 1/4 cup olive oil
- 2 Tbsp lemon juice
- 1 tsp Dijon mustard
- 1 tsp honey
- Salt and pepper to taste

DIRECTIONS:

1. In a medium saucepan, combine quinoa and water. Bring to a boil, then reduce heat and simmer for 15 minutes or until quinoa is cooked.
2. In a large bowl, combine cooked quinoa, kale, carrots, dried cranberries, sunflower seeds, and feta cheese.
3. In a small bowl, whisk together olive oil, lemon juice, Dijon mustard, honey, salt, and pepper.
4. Pour the dressing over the salad and toss to combine.
5. Serve immediately.

TIPS:

- Massage the kale with a little olive oil before adding to the salad to soften it.
- Add grilled shrimp for extra protein.

NUTRITIONAL VALUES: Calories: 280, Fat: 14g, Carbs: 32g, Protein: 8g, Sugar: 10g

ASIAN-INSPIRED SESAME TUNA SALAD

PREPARATION TIME: 15 min
COOKING TIME: 10 min
MODE OF COOKING: Stovetop
SERVINGS: 4

INGREDIENTS:

- 2 ahi tuna steaks
- 1 Tbsp sesame oil
- Salt and pepper to taste

- 4 cups mixed greens
- 1 cup shredded red cabbage
- 1/2 cup edamame, shelled
- 1/2 cup shredded carrots
- 1 avocado, sliced
- 2 Tbsp sesame seeds

Dressing:
- 1/4 cup soy sauce or tamari
- 2 Tbsp rice vinegar
- 1 Tbsp sesame oil
- 1 tsp honey
- 1 tsp grated ginger

DIRECTIONS:
1. Heat sesame oil in a skillet over medium-high heat.
2. Season tuna steaks with salt and pepper.
3. Sear tuna steaks for 1-2 minutes on each side, or until desired doneness. Let rest, then slice thinly.
4. In a large bowl, combine mixed greens, red cabbage, edamame, shredded carrots, and avocado.
5. In a small bowl, whisk together soy sauce, rice vinegar, sesame oil, honey, and grated ginger.
6. Pour the dressing over the salad and toss to combine.
7. Top with sesame seeds and sliced tuna.
8. Serve immediately.

TIPS:
- Use a mandoline to shred the cabbage and carrots quickly.
- Add a sprinkle of chopped cilantro for extra flavor.

NUTRITIONAL VALUES: Calories: 350, Fat: 20g, Carbs: 18g, Protein: 25g, Sugar: 7g

---

ROASTED BEET AND GOAT CHEESE SALAD

PREPARATION TIME: 15 min
COOKING TIME: 40 min
MODE OF COOKING: Roasting
SERVINGS: 4
INGREDIENTS:
- 4 medium beets, scrubbed and trimmed
- 1 Tbsp olive oil
- Salt and pepper to taste
- 6 cups arugula
- 1/4 cup walnuts, toasted
- 1/4 cup goat cheese, crumbled

Dressing:
- 1/4 cup balsamic vinegar
- 2 Tbsp olive oil
- 1 tsp Dijon mustard
- 1 tsp honey
- Salt and pepper to taste

DIRECTIONS:
1. Preheat oven to 400°F (200°C).
2. Wrap each beet in foil and place on a baking sheet. Roast for 35-40 minutes, or until tender.
3. Allow beets to cool, then peel and cut into wedges.
4. In a large bowl, combine arugula, roasted beets, walnuts, and goat cheese.
5. In a small bowl, whisk together balsamic vinegar, olive oil, Dijon mustard, honey, salt, and pepper.
6. Pour the dressing over the salad and toss to combine.
7. Serve immediately.

TIPS:
- Wear gloves when peeling beets to avoid staining your hands.
- Add sliced red onion for extra crunch.

NUTRITIONAL VALUES: Calories: 220, Fat: 14g, Carbs: 20g, Protein: 5g, Sugar: 10g

DIVERSE PREPARATIONS OF VEGETABLES: FROM ROASTING TO RAW

ROASTED BRUSSELS SPROUTS WITH BALSAMIC GLAZE

PREPARATION TIME: 10 min
COOKING TIME: 25 min
MODE OF COOKING: Roasting
SERVINGS: 4
INGREDIENTS:

- 1 lb Brussels sprouts, trimmed and halved
- 2 Tbsp olive oil
- Salt and pepper to taste
- 1/4 cup balsamic vinegar
- 1 Tbsp honey

DIRECTIONS:

1. Preheat oven to 400°F (200°C).
2. Toss Brussels sprouts with olive oil, salt, and pepper.
3. Spread out on a baking sheet and roast for 20-25 minutes, until tender and caramelized.
4. In a small saucepan, heat balsamic vinegar and honey over medium heat until reduced to a glaze, about 5 minutes.
5. Drizzle the balsamic glaze over the roasted Brussels sprouts and serve.

TIPS:

- Add a sprinkle of crushed red pepper for a spicy kick.
- Top with toasted pine nuts for extra texture.

NUTRITIONAL VALUES: Calories: 110, Fat: 7g, Carbs: 12g, Protein: 3g, Sugar: 6g

RAW CARROT AND CUCUMBER SALAD

PREPARATION TIME: 15 min
COOKING TIME: N/A
MODE OF COOKING: Raw
SERVINGS: 4
INGREDIENTS:

- 3 large carrots, peeled and shredded
- 1 large cucumber, thinly sliced
- 1/4 cup red onion, thinly sliced
- 2 Tbsp fresh dill, chopped
- 2 Tbsp olive oil
- 1 Tbsp lemon juice
- Salt and pepper to taste

DIRECTIONS:

1. In a large bowl, combine carrots, cucumber, red onion, and dill.
2. In a small bowl, whisk together olive oil, lemon juice, salt, and pepper.
3. Pour the dressing over the vegetables and toss to combine.
4. Serve immediately.

TIPS:

- Add a handful of chopped fresh mint for extra freshness.
- Serve with grilled fish for a light meal.

NUTRITIONAL VALUES: Calories: 80, Fat: 6g, Carbs: 7g, Protein: 1g, Sugar: 3g

GARLIC PARMESAN ROASTED CAULIFLOWER

PREPARATION TIME: 10 min
COOKING TIME: 30 min
MODE OF COOKING: Roasting
SERVINGS: 4
INGREDIENTS:

- 1 head cauliflower, cut into florets
- 3 Tbsp olive oil
- 3 cloves garlic, minced
- 1/4 cup grated Parmesan cheese
- Salt and pepper to taste
- 1 Tbsp chopped fresh parsley

DIRECTIONS:

1. Preheat oven to 425°F (220°C).
2. In a large bowl, toss cauliflower florets with olive oil, garlic, salt, and pepper.
3. Spread out on a baking sheet and roast for 25-30 minutes, until golden and tender.
4. Sprinkle with Parmesan cheese and parsley before serving.

TIPS:

- Add a squeeze of lemon juice for extra flavor.
- Top with red pepper flakes for a bit of heat.

NUTRITIONAL VALUES: Calories: 140, Fat: 10g, Carbs: 10g, Protein: 4g, Sugar: 2g

RAW KALE AND AVOCADO SALAD

PREPARATION TIME: 15 min
COOKING TIME: N/A
MODE OF COOKING: Raw
SERVINGS: 4
INGREDIENTS:

- 4 cups kale, chopped
- 1 avocado, diced
- 1/4 cup red onion, thinly sliced
- 1/4 cup sunflower seeds
- 1 Tbsp olive oil
- 1 Tbsp lemon juice
- Salt and pepper to taste

DIRECTIONS:

1. In a large bowl, massage kale with olive oil and lemon juice for 2-3 minutes until softened.
2. Add avocado, red onion, and sunflower seeds to the bowl.
3. Toss to combine and season with salt and pepper.
4. Serve immediately.

TIPS:

- Add a sprinkle of feta cheese for added flavor.
- Use baby kale for a more tender salad.

NUTRITIONAL VALUES: Calories: 160, Fat: 13g, Carbs: 10g, Protein: 3g, Sugar: 1g

ROASTED EGGPLANT WITH TAHINI DRIZZLE

PREPARATION TIME: 10 min
COOKING TIME: 25 min
MODE OF COOKING: Roasting
SERVINGS: 4
INGREDIENTS:

- 2 medium eggplants, sliced into rounds
- 3 Tbsp olive oil
- Salt and pepper to taste
- 2 Tbsp tahini
- 1 Tbsp lemon juice
- 1 clove garlic, minced
- 2-3 Tbsp water

DIRECTIONS:

1. Preheat oven to 425°F (220°C).
2. Brush eggplant slices with olive oil and season with salt and pepper.
3. Arrange on a baking sheet and roast for 20-25 minutes, until golden and tender.
4. In a small bowl, whisk together tahini, lemon juice, garlic, and water until smooth.
5. Drizzle the tahini sauce over the roasted eggplant and serve.

TIPS:

- Sprinkle with chopped fresh parsley for added color.
- Serve as a side dish or as part of a mezze platter.

NUTRITIONAL VALUES: Calories: 180, Fat: 14g, Carbs: 12g, Protein: 3g, Sugar: 2g

RAW ZUCCHINI NOODLES WITH PESTO

PREPARATION TIME: 15 min
COOKING TIME: N/A
MODE OF COOKING: Raw
SERVINGS: 4

INGREDIENTS:

- 4 medium zucchinis, spiralized
- 1/2 cup cherry tomatoes, halved
- 1/4 cup pine nuts, toasted
- 1/4 cup grated Parmesan cheese

Pesto:

- 2 cups fresh basil leaves
- 1/4 cup pine nuts
- 1/4 cup grated Parmesan cheese
- 1 clove garlic
- 1/2 cup olive oil
- Salt and pepper to taste

DIRECTIONS:

1. In a food processor, combine basil, pine nuts, Parmesan cheese, and garlic.
2. Pulse until finely chopped.
3. With the processor running, slowly add olive oil until the mixture is smooth.
4. Season with salt and pepper.
5. In a large bowl, toss spiralized zucchini with pesto, cherry tomatoes, pine nuts, and grated Parmesan.
6. Serve immediately.

TIPS:

- Add grilled chicken or shrimp for extra protein.
- Use a spiralizer to make uniform zucchini noodles.

NUTRITIONAL VALUES: Calories: 220, Fat: 18g, Carbs: 10g, Protein: 6g, Sugar: 4g

HOMEMADE CONDIMENTS AND DRESSINGS

CLASSIC BALSAMIC VINAIGRETTE

PREPARATION TIME: 5 min
COOKING TIME: N/A
MODE OF COOKING: Mixing
SERVINGS: 8 (2 Tbsp per serving)
INGREDIENTS:

- 1/4 cup balsamic vinegar
- 3/4 cup extra virgin olive oil
- 1 Tbsp Dijon mustard
- 1 clove garlic, minced
- 1 tsp honey
- Salt and pepper to taste

DIRECTIONS:

1. In a small bowl, whisk together balsamic vinegar, Dijon mustard, garlic, honey, salt, and pepper.
2. Slowly drizzle in the olive oil while whisking continuously until emulsified.
3. Adjust seasoning to taste.
4. Store in an airtight container in the refrigerator for up to one week.

TIPS:

- Shake well before each use.
- Add a splash of lemon juice for extra tang.

NUTRITIONAL VALUES: Calories: 170, Fat: 18g, Carbs: 2g, Protein: 0g, Sugar: 1g

CREAMY AVOCADO DRESSING

PREPARATION TIME: 10 min
COOKING TIME: N/A
MODE OF COOKING: Blending
SERVINGS: 6 (2 Tbsp per serving)
INGREDIENTS:

- 1 ripe avocado
- 1/4 cup plain Greek yogurt
- 2 Tbsp fresh lime juice
- 1 clove garlic, minced
- 2 Tbsp cilantro, chopped
- 1/4 cup water (adjust for desired consistency)
- Salt and pepper to taste

DIRECTIONS:

1. In a blender, combine avocado, Greek yogurt, lime juice, garlic, cilantro, water, salt, and pepper.
2. Blend until smooth, adding more water as needed for desired consistency.
3. Adjust seasoning to taste.
4. Store in an airtight container in the refrigerator for up to three days.

TIPS:

- Use as a dip for vegetables or a spread for sandwiches.
- Add a pinch of cumin for a smoky flavor.

NUTRITIONAL VALUES: Calories: 60, Fat: 5g, Carbs: 4g, Protein: 2g, Sugar: 1g

LEMON TAHINI DRESSING

PREPARATION TIME: 5 min
COOKING TIME: N/A
MODE OF COOKING: Mixing
SERVINGS: 8 (2 Tbsp per serving)
INGREDIENTS:

- 1/4 cup tahini
- 1/4 cup fresh lemon juice
- 2 Tbsp water
- 1 Tbsp olive oil
- 1 clove garlic, minced
- 1 tsp maple syrup
- Salt and pepper to taste

DIRECTIONS:

1. In a small bowl, whisk together tahini, lemon juice, water, olive oil, garlic, and maple syrup.
2. Season with salt and pepper to taste.
3. Adjust consistency with more water if needed.
4. Store in an airtight container in the refrigerator for up to one week.

TIPS:

- Use as a sauce for grilled vegetables or salads.
- Add a dash of cayenne pepper for a spicy kick.

NUTRITIONAL VALUES: Calories: 70, Fat: 6g, Carbs: 3g, Protein: 2g, Sugar: 1g

SPICY PEANUT DRESSING

PREPARATION TIME: 5 min
COOKING TIME: N/A
MODE OF COOKING: Mixing
SERVINGS: 6 (2 Tbsp per serving)
INGREDIENTS:

- 1/4 cup natural peanut butter
- 2 Tbsp rice vinegar
- 1 Tbsp soy sauce or tamari
- 1 Tbsp honey
- 1 clove garlic, minced
- 1 tsp grated ginger
- 1-2 Tbsp water (to adjust consistency)
- 1/2 tsp red pepper flakes (optional)

DIRECTIONS:

1. In a small bowl, whisk together peanut butter, rice vinegar, soy sauce, honey, garlic, ginger, and water until smooth.
2. Add red pepper flakes if using and mix well.
3. Adjust consistency with more water if needed.
4. Store in an airtight container in the refrigerator for up to one week.

TIPS:

- Great as a dip for spring rolls or drizzled over salads.
- Use as a marinade for chicken or tofu.

NUTRITIONAL VALUES: Calories: 90, Fat: 7g, Carbs: 4g, Protein: 3g, Sugar: 3g

HERB AND GARLIC YOGURT DRESSING

PREPARATION TIME: 5 min
COOKING TIME: N/A
MODE OF COOKING: Mixing
SERVINGS: 8 (2 Tbsp per serving)
INGREDIENTS:

- 1 cup plain Greek yogurt
- 1/4 cup fresh parsley, chopped
- 1/4 cup fresh dill, chopped
- 1 clove garlic, minced
- 1 Tbsp lemon juice
- 1 tsp honey
- Salt and pepper to taste

DIRECTIONS:

1. In a small bowl, whisk together Greek yogurt, parsley, dill, garlic, lemon juice, and honey.
2. Season with salt and pepper to taste.
3. Store in an airtight container in the refrigerator for up to one week.

TIPS:

- Use as a dip for fresh vegetables or a dressing for salads.
- Add chopped chives for extra flavor.

NUTRITIONAL VALUES: Calories: 30, Fat: 1g, Carbs: 2g, Protein: 4g, Sugar: 1g

HONEY MUSTARD DRESSING

PREPARATION TIME: 5 min
COOKING TIME: N/A
MODE OF COOKING: Mixing
SERVINGS: 8 (2 Tbsp per serving)

INGREDIENTS:

- 1/4 cup Dijon mustard
- 2 Tbsp honey
- 2 Tbsp apple cider vinegar

- 1/4 cup olive oil
- Salt and pepper to taste

DIRECTIONS:

1. In a small bowl, whisk together Dijon mustard, honey, apple cider vinegar, salt, and pepper.
2. Slowly drizzle in olive oil while whisking continuously until emulsified.
3. Store in an airtight container in the refrigerator for up to one week.

TIPS:

- Perfect for drizzling over salads or as a dip for chicken tenders.
- Add a splash of lemon juice for extra zest.

NUTRITIONAL VALUES: Calories: 110, Fat: 9g, Carbs: 7g, Protein: 0g, Sugar: 6g

7. SEAFOOD SPECIALTIES

TECHNIQUES FOR PREPARING FISH: GRILLING AND BAKING

GRILLED LEMON HERB SALMON

PREPARATION TIME: 10 min
COOKING TIME: 15 min
MODE OF COOKING: Grilling
SERVINGS: 4
INGREDIENTS:

- 4 salmon fillets (6 oz each)
- 2 Tbsp olive oil
- 2 Tbsp fresh lemon juice
- 1 tsp lemon zest
- 2 garlic cloves, minced
- 2 Tbsp fresh parsley, chopped
- Salt and pepper to taste
- Lemon slices for garnish

DIRECTIONS:

1. Preheat the grill to medium-high heat.
2. In a small bowl, mix olive oil, lemon juice, lemon zest, garlic, parsley, salt, and pepper.
3. Brush the salmon fillets with the mixture.
4. Place salmon fillets on the grill, skin-side down.
5. Grill for 6-7 minutes per side, or until the salmon is opaque and flakes easily with a fork.
6. Serve immediately, garnished with lemon slices.

TIPS:

- Use a fish grill basket to prevent the salmon from sticking.
- Marinate the salmon for 30 minutes for extra flavor.

NUTRITIONAL VALUES: Calories: 300, Fat: 18g, Carbs: 1g, Protein: 33g, Sugar: 0g

BAKED HERB-CRUSTED COD

PREPARATION TIME: 15 min
COOKING TIME: 20 min
MODE OF COOKING: Baking
SERVINGS: 4
INGREDIENTS:

- 4 cod fillets (6 oz each)
- 1/2 cup almond flour
- 1/4 cup grated Parmesan cheese
- 1 tsp dried thyme
- 1 tsp dried oregano
- 1 tsp dried basil
- 2 Tbsp olive oil
- Salt and pepper to taste
- Lemon wedges for serving

DIRECTIONS:

1. Preheat oven to 400°F (200°C).
2. In a bowl, combine almond flour, Parmesan cheese, thyme, oregano, basil, salt, and pepper.
3. Brush cod fillets with olive oil.
4. Dredge each fillet in the almond flour mixture, coating evenly.
5. Place on a baking sheet lined with parchment paper.
6. Bake for 15-20 minutes, or until the fish is golden and flakes easily with a fork.
7. Serve with lemon wedges.

TIPS:

- Use fresh herbs if available for a more vibrant flavor.
- Serve with a side of roasted vegetables.

NUTRITIONAL VALUES: Calories: 280, Fat: 16g, Carbs: 5g, Protein: 30g, Sugar: 1g

GRILLED MAHI-MAHI WITH MANGO SALSA

PREPARATION TIME: 15 min
COOKING TIME: 10 min
MODE OF COOKING: Grilling
SERVINGS: 4
INGREDIENTS:

- 4 mahi-mahi fillets (6 oz each)
- 2 Tbsp olive oil
- 1 tsp chili powder
- 1/2 tsp garlic powder
- Salt and pepper to taste

Mango Salsa:

- 1 ripe mango, diced
- 1/2 red bell pepper, diced
- 1/4 cup red onion, finely chopped
- 1 jalapeño, seeded and minced
- 2 Tbsp fresh cilantro, chopped
- 1 Tbsp fresh lime juice
- Salt to taste

DIRECTIONS:

1. Preheat the grill to medium-high heat.
2. In a small bowl, mix olive oil, chili powder, garlic powder, salt, and pepper.
3. Brush the mahi-mahi fillets with the mixture.
4. Grill the fillets for 4-5 minutes per side, or until the fish is opaque and flakes easily with a fork.
5. In a separate bowl, combine all salsa ingredients.
6. Serve the grilled mahi-mahi topped with mango salsa.

TIPS:

- Use pineapple instead of mango for a different twist.
- Marinate the fish for 20 minutes to enhance the flavor.

NUTRITIONAL VALUES: Calories: 260, Fat: 12g, Carbs: 10g, Protein: 30g, Sugar: 6g

---

BAKED DIJON-CRUSTED TILAPIA

PREPARATION TIME: 10 min
COOKING TIME: 20 min
MODE OF COOKING: Baking
SERVINGS: 4
INGREDIENTS:

- 4 tilapia fillets (6 oz each)
- 1/4 cup Dijon mustard
- 1/4 cup mayonnaise
- 1/4 cup grated Parmesan cheese
- 1/2 cup panko breadcrumbs
- 2 Tbsp fresh parsley, chopped
- Salt and pepper to taste
- Lemon wedges for serving

DIRECTIONS:

1. Preheat oven to 375°F (190°C).
2. In a small bowl, mix Dijon mustard, mayonnaise, and Parmesan cheese.
3. Spread the mixture evenly over each tilapia fillet.
4. Sprinkle panko breadcrumbs and parsley over the top.
5. Place on a baking sheet lined with parchment paper.
6. Bake for 15-20 minutes, or until the fish is golden and flakes easily with a fork.
7. Serve with lemon wedges.

TIPS:

- Add a pinch of paprika for a smoky flavor.
- Serve with a side salad for a light meal.

NUTRITIONAL VALUES: Calories: 280, Fat: 16g, Carbs: 8g, Protein: 28g, Sugar: 1g

---

GRILLED SWORDFISH WITH HERB BUTTER

PREPARATION TIME: 10 min
COOKING TIME: 10 min
MODE OF COOKING: Grilling
SERVINGS: 4
INGREDIENTS:

- 4 swordfish steaks (6 oz each)
- 2 Tbsp olive oil
- Salt and pepper to taste
- 1/4 cup unsalted butter, softened
- 1 Tbsp fresh lemon juice
- 1 Tbsp fresh parsley, chopped
- 1 Tbsp fresh dill, chopped

DIRECTIONS:

1. Preheat the grill to medium-high heat.
2. Brush swordfish steaks with olive oil and season with salt and pepper.
3. Grill the steaks for 4-5 minutes per side, or until the fish is opaque and flakes easily with a fork.
4. In a small bowl, mix softened butter, lemon juice, parsley, and dill.
5. Top each steak with a dollop of herb butter before serving.

TIPS:

- Serve with grilled asparagus or a fresh green salad.
- Use a fish basket to prevent sticking.

NUTRITIONAL VALUES: Calories: 360, Fat: 24g, Carbs: 0g, Protein: 34g, Sugar: 0g

---

BAKED PESTO CRUSTED HALIBUT

PREPARATION TIME: 15 min
COOKING TIME: 20 min
MODE OF COOKING: Baking
SERVINGS: 4

INGREDIENTS:

- 4 halibut fillets (6 oz each)
- 1/4 cup basil pesto
- 1/4 cup panko breadcrumbs
- 2 Tbsp grated Parmesan cheese

- 1 Tbsp olive oil
- Salt and pepper to taste
- Lemon wedges for serving

DIRECTIONS:

1. Preheat oven to 400°F (200°C).
2. Spread basil pesto evenly over each halibut fillet.
3. In a small bowl, mix panko breadcrumbs, Parmesan cheese, and olive oil.
4. Sprinkle the breadcrumb mixture over the pesto-coated fillets.
5. Place on a baking sheet lined with parchment paper.
6. Bake for 15-20 minutes, or until the fish is golden and flakes easily with a fork.
7. Serve with lemon wedges.

TIPS:

- Use homemade pesto for a fresher taste.
- Serve with roasted vegetables or a quinoa salad.

NUTRITIONAL VALUES: Calories: 340, Fat: 20g, Carbs: 6g, Protein: 34g, Sugar: 0g

FISH AND SEAFOOD SOUPS AND STEWS

MEDITERRANEAN FISH STEW

PREPARATION TIME: 15 min
COOKING TIME: 30 min
MODE OF COOKING: Stovetop
SERVINGS: 4
INGREDIENTS:

- 1 lb firm white fish (cod or halibut), cut into chunks
- 2 Tbsp olive oil
- 1 onion, chopped
- 2 garlic cloves, minced
- 1 red bell pepper, chopped
- 1 can (14.5 oz) diced tomatoes
- 1 cup fish stock or vegetable broth
- 1/2 cup dry white wine
- 1 tsp dried oregano
- 1 tsp dried thyme
- 1/4 cup chopped fresh parsley
- Salt and pepper to taste
- Lemon wedges for serving

DIRECTIONS:

1. Heat olive oil in a large pot over medium heat. Add onion and garlic, sauté until softened.
2. Add red bell pepper and cook for another 5 minutes.
3. Stir in diced tomatoes, fish stock, white wine, oregano, and thyme. Bring to a simmer.
4. Add the fish chunks and cook for 10-12 minutes until the fish is cooked through.
5. Season with salt and pepper to taste. Stir in fresh parsley.
6. Serve hot with lemon wedges on the side.

TIPS:

- Add a pinch of red pepper flakes for a spicy kick.
- Serve with a side of crusty bread (optional).

NUTRITIONAL VALUES: Calories: 220, Fat: 10g, Carbs: 8g, Protein: 24g, Sugar: 4g

CREAMY SEAFOOD CHOWDER

PREPARATION TIME: 20 min
COOKING TIME: 30 min
MODE OF COOKING: Stovetop
SERVINGS: 4
INGREDIENTS:

- 1 Tbsp butter
- 1 onion, chopped
- 2 celery stalks, chopped
- 2 garlic cloves, minced
- 2 cups fish stock or vegetable broth
- 1 cup heavy cream
- 1/2 cup dry white wine
- 1 lb mixed seafood (shrimp, scallops, and fish), cut into bite-sized pieces
- 1 cup cauliflower florets, chopped
- 1 bay leaf
- 1 tsp dried thyme
- Salt and pepper to taste
- Fresh parsley for garnish

DIRECTIONS:

1. In a large pot, melt butter over medium heat. Add onion, celery, and garlic, sauté until softened.
2. Add fish stock, heavy cream, white wine, cauliflower, bay leaf, and thyme. Bring to a simmer.
3. Cook for 15-20 minutes until cauliflower is tender.
4. Add mixed seafood and cook for another 5-7 minutes until seafood is cooked through.
5. Season with salt and pepper to taste. Remove bay leaf.
6. Serve hot, garnished with fresh parsley.

TIPS:

- Use coconut milk instead of cream for a dairy-free option.
- Add a splash of hot sauce for extra heat.

NUTRITIONAL VALUES: Calories: 300, Fat: 20g, Carbs: 10g, Protein: 20g, Sugar: 3g

---

SPICY SHRIMP AND TOMATO STEW

PREPARATION TIME: 15 min
COOKING TIME: 25 min
MODE OF COOKING: Stovetop
SERVINGS: 4
INGREDIENTS:

- 1 lb shrimp, peeled and deveined
- 2 Tbsp olive oil
- 1 onion, chopped
- 2 garlic cloves, minced
- 1 red bell pepper, chopped
- 1 can (14.5 oz) diced tomatoes
- 1 cup fish stock or vegetable broth
- 1/2 cup dry white wine
- 1 tsp smoked paprika
- 1/2 tsp cayenne pepper
- 1/4 cup chopped fresh cilantro
- Salt and pepper to taste
- Lime wedges for serving

DIRECTIONS:

1. Heat olive oil in a large pot over medium heat. Add onion and garlic, sauté until softened.
2. Add red bell pepper and cook for another 5 minutes.
3. Stir in diced tomatoes, fish stock, white wine, smoked paprika, and cayenne pepper. Bring to a simmer.
4. Add shrimp and cook for 5-7 minutes until shrimp is cooked through.
5. Season with salt and pepper to taste. Stir in fresh cilantro.
6. Serve hot with lime wedges on the side.

TIPS:

- Add a can of black beans for added protein and fiber.
- Serve over cauliflower rice for a low-carb option.

NUTRITIONAL VALUES: Calories: 230, Fat: 12g, Carbs: 10g, Protein: 20g, Sugar: 4g

---

LEMON DILL SALMON CHOWDER

PREPARATION TIME: 15 min
COOKING TIME: 25 min
MODE OF COOKING: Stovetop
SERVINGS: 4
INGREDIENTS:

- 1 Tbsp olive oil
- 1 onion, chopped
- 2 garlic cloves, minced
- 2 celery stalks, chopped
- 1 cup cauliflower florets, chopped
- 4 cups fish stock or vegetable broth
- 1/2 cup heavy cream
- 1 lb salmon fillets, skin removed, cut into chunks
- 1 tsp dried dill
- Juice and zest of 1 lemon
- Salt and pepper to taste
- Fresh dill for garnish

DIRECTIONS:

1. Heat olive oil in a large pot over medium heat. Add onion, garlic, and celery, sauté until softened.
2. Add cauliflower and cook for another 5 minutes.
3. Stir in fish stock and bring to a simmer. Cook for 10-12 minutes until cauliflower is tender.
4. Add heavy cream, salmon, dried dill, lemon juice, and zest. Cook for another 5-7 minutes

until salmon is cooked through.
5. Season with salt and pepper to taste.
6. Serve hot, garnished with fresh dill.

TIPS:
- Add a handful of spinach for extra greens.
- Use coconut milk instead of cream for a dairy-free option.

NUTRITIONAL VALUES: Calories: 280, Fat: 18g, Carbs: 8g, Protein: 22g, Sugar: 2g

THAI COCONUT SHRIMP SOUP

PREPARATION TIME: 15 min
COOKING TIME: 20 min
MODE OF COOKING: Stovetop
SERVINGS: 4
INGREDIENTS:
- 1 Tbsp coconut oil
- 1 onion, chopped
- 2 garlic cloves, minced
- 1 Tbsp fresh ginger, grated
- 1 red bell pepper, sliced
- 1 can (14 oz) coconut milk
- 4 cups fish stock or vegetable broth
- 1 Tbsp red curry paste
- 1 lb shrimp, peeled and deveined
- 2 Tbsp fish sauce
- Juice of 1 lime
- 1/4 cup fresh cilantro, chopped
- Salt and pepper to taste

DIRECTIONS:
1. Heat coconut oil in a large pot over medium heat. Add onion, garlic, and ginger, sauté until fragrant.
2. Add red bell pepper and cook for another 5 minutes.
3. Stir in coconut milk, fish stock, and red curry paste. Bring to a simmer.
4. Add shrimp and cook for 5-7 minutes until shrimp is cooked through.
5. Stir in fish sauce, lime juice, and cilantro.
6. Season with salt and pepper to taste.
7. Serve hot.

TIPS:
- Add mushrooms for extra texture.
- Serve with a side of lime wedges.

NUTRITIONAL VALUES: Calories: 300, Fat: 20g, Carbs: 10g, Protein: 22g, Sugar: 4g

SPANISH SEAFOOD STEW

PREPARATION TIME: 20 min
COOKING TIME: 35 min
MODE OF COOKING: Stovetop
SERVINGS: 4
INGREDIENTS:
- 2 Tbsp olive oil
- 1 onion, chopped
- 2 garlic cloves, minced
- 1 red bell pepper, chopped
- 1 green bell pepper, chopped
- 1 can (14.5 oz) diced tomatoes
- 4 cups fish stock or vegetable broth
- 1/2 cup dry white wine
- 1 tsp smoked paprika
- 1/2 tsp saffron threads
- 1 lb mixed seafood (mussels, shrimp, and fish), cleaned and cut into bite-sized pieces
- 1/4 cup fresh parsley, chopped
- Salt and pepper to taste

DIRECTIONS:
1. Heat olive oil in a large pot over medium heat. Add onion, garlic, and bell peppers, sauté until softened.
2. Stir in diced tomatoes, fish stock, white wine, smoked paprika, and saffron threads. Bring to a simmer.
3. Cook for 20 minutes, allowing the flavors to meld.
4. Add mixed seafood and cook for another 5-7 minutes until seafood is cooked through.
5. Season with salt and pepper to taste. Stir in fresh parsley.
6. Serve hot.

TIPS:
- Serve with a side of crusty bread (optional).
- Add a pinch of red pepper flakes for a spicy kick.

NUTRITIONAL VALUES: Calories: 320, Fat: 14g, Carbs: 12g, Protein: 36g, Sugar: 6g

GARLIC BUTTER SHRIMP

PREPARATION TIME: 10 min
COOKING TIME: 10 min
MODE OF COOKING: Stovetop
SERVINGS: 4
INGREDIENTS:

- 1 lb large shrimp, peeled and deveined
- 3 Tbsp unsalted butter
- 4 garlic cloves, minced
- 1/4 cup chicken broth or white wine
- 1 Tbsp lemon juice
- 2 Tbsp fresh parsley, chopped
- Salt and pepper to taste
- Lemon wedges for serving

DIRECTIONS:

1. Heat butter in a large skillet over medium-high heat.
2. Add garlic and sauté for 1-2 minutes until fragrant.
3. Add shrimp and cook for 2-3 minutes on each side until pink and opaque.
4. Pour in chicken broth or white wine and lemon juice. Cook for another 2-3 minutes until the sauce is slightly reduced.
5. Season with salt and pepper, and stir in fresh parsley.
6. Serve immediately with lemon wedges.

TIPS:

- Serve over cauliflower rice or zucchini noodles for a low-carb option.
- Add a pinch of red pepper flakes for a bit of heat.

NUTRITIONAL VALUES: Calories: 220, Fat: 12g, Carbs: 2g, Protein: 23g, Sugar: 0g

BAKED LEMON HERB TILAPIA

PREPARATION TIME: 10 min
COOKING TIME: 15 min
MODE OF COOKING: Baking
SERVINGS: 4
INGREDIENTS:

- 4 tilapia fillets (6 oz each)
- 2 Tbsp olive oil
- 2 Tbsp lemon juice
- 1 tsp lemon zest
- 2 garlic cloves, minced
- 1 tsp dried basil
- 1 tsp dried oregano
- Salt and pepper to taste
- Fresh parsley for garnish

DIRECTIONS:

1. Preheat oven to 375°F (190°C).
2. In a small bowl, mix olive oil, lemon juice, lemon zest, garlic, basil, oregano, salt, and pepper.
3. Place tilapia fillets in a baking dish and brush with the lemon herb mixture.
4. Bake for 12-15 minutes, or until the fish is opaque and flakes easily with a fork.
5. Garnish with fresh parsley and serve immediately.

TIPS:

- Serve with steamed broccoli or a mixed green salad.
- Add a side of roasted sweet potatoes for a complete meal.

NUTRITIONAL VALUES: Calories: 180, Fat: 10g, Carbs: 1g, Protein: 21g, Sugar: 0g

MEDITERRANEAN BAKED COD

PREPARATION TIME: 15 min
COOKING TIME: 20 min
MODE OF COOKING: Baking
SERVINGS: 4

INGREDIENTS:

- 4 cod fillets (6 oz each)
- 2 Tbsp olive oil
- 1 can (14.5 oz) diced tomatoes

- 1/2 cup Kalamata olives, pitted and halved
- 1/4 cup red onion, thinly sliced
- 1 tsp dried oregano
- 1 tsp dried thyme
- Salt and pepper to taste
- Fresh basil for garnish

DIRECTIONS:
1. Preheat oven to 400°F (200°C).
2. In a baking dish, combine diced tomatoes, olives, red onion, oregano, thyme, salt, and pepper.
3. Place cod fillets on top of the tomato mixture and drizzle with olive oil.
4. Bake for 20 minutes, or until the fish is opaque and flakes easily with a fork.
5. Garnish with fresh basil and serve.

TIPS:
- Serve with a side of quinoa or cauliflower rice.
- Add a squeeze of lemon juice for extra brightness.

NUTRITIONAL VALUES: Calories: 220, Fat: 10g, Carbs: 6g, Protein: 26g, Sugar: 3g

---

SPICY GRILLED MAHI-MAHI

PREPARATION TIME: 10 min
COOKING TIME: 15 min
MODE OF COOKING: Grilling
SERVINGS: 4
INGREDIENTS:
- 4 mahi-mahi fillets (6 oz each)
- 2 Tbsp olive oil
- 1 tsp paprika
- 1 tsp garlic powder
- 1/2 tsp cayenne pepper
- Salt and pepper to taste
- Lime wedges for serving

DIRECTIONS:
1. Preheat grill to medium-high heat.
2. In a small bowl, mix olive oil, paprika, garlic powder, cayenne pepper, salt, and pepper.
3. Brush mahi-mahi fillets with the spice mixture.
4. Grill fillets for 6-7 minutes per side, or until the fish is opaque and flakes easily with a fork.
5. Serve immediately with lime wedges.

TIPS:
- Serve with grilled vegetables or a fresh green salad.
- Use the spice mixture on other types of fish for variety.

NUTRITIONAL VALUES: Calories: 200, Fat: 10g, Carbs: 1g, Protein: 26g, Sugar: 0g

---

LEMON GARLIC SCALLOPS

PREPARATION TIME: 10 min
COOKING TIME: 10 min
MODE OF COOKING: Stovetop
SERVINGS: 4
INGREDIENTS:
- 1 lb sea scallops
- 2 Tbsp olive oil
- 3 garlic cloves, minced
- 1/4 cup chicken broth or white wine
- 2 Tbsp lemon juice
- 1 Tbsp fresh parsley, chopped
- Salt and pepper to taste
- Lemon wedges for serving

DIRECTIONS:
1. Pat scallops dry with a paper towel and season with salt and pepper.
2. Heat olive oil in a large skillet over medium-high heat.
3. Add scallops and cook for 2-3 minutes on each side until golden and opaque.
4. Remove scallops from the skillet and set aside.
5. Add garlic to the skillet and sauté for 1 minute.
6. Pour in chicken broth or white wine and lemon juice, and cook for another 2-3 minutes until the sauce is slightly reduced.
7. Return scallops to the skillet and coat with the sauce.
8. Serve immediately, garnished with fresh parsley and lemon wedges.

TIPS:
- Serve over cauliflower mash or steamed asparagus.
- Add a pinch of red pepper flakes for a spicy touch.

NUTRITIONAL VALUES: Calories: 240, Fat: 10g, Carbs: 3g, Protein: 32g, Sugar: 0g

PREPARATION TIME: 10 min
COOKING TIME: 15 min
MODE OF COOKING: Stovetop
SERVINGS: 4
INGREDIENTS:

- 1 lb shrimp, peeled and deveined
- 2 Tbsp coconut oil
- 2 garlic cloves, minced
- 1 red bell pepper, sliced
- 1 yellow bell pepper, sliced
- 1 cup snap peas
- 2 Tbsp soy sauce or tamari
- 1 Tbsp fish sauce
- 1 Tbsp fresh lime juice
- 1/4 cup fresh basil leaves, chopped
- Salt and pepper to taste

DIRECTIONS:

1. Heat coconut oil in a large skillet over medium-high heat.
2. Add garlic and sauté for 1-2 minutes until fragrant.
3. Add shrimp and cook for 2-3 minutes until pink and opaque. Remove shrimp from the skillet and set aside.
4. Add bell peppers and snap peas to the skillet, and stir-fry for 5-7 minutes until tender-crisp.
5. Return shrimp to the skillet and stir in soy sauce, fish sauce, and lime juice.
6. Cook for another 2-3 minutes until heated through.
7. Stir in fresh basil and season with salt and pepper.
8. Serve immediately.

TIPS:

- Serve over cauliflower rice or zucchini noodles for a low-carb option.
- Add sliced chili peppers for extra heat.

NUTRITIONAL VALUES: Calories: 250, Fat: 12g, Carbs: 8g, Protein: 30g, Sugar: 3g

8. MAIN COURSES: POULTRY-BASED DISHES

TRADITIONAL CHICKEN DISHES

HERB-ROASTED CHICKEN

PREPARATION TIME: 15 min
COOKING TIME: 1 hr 20 min
MODE OF COOKING: Roasting
SERVINGS: 6
INGREDIENTS:

- 1 whole chicken (4-5 lb)
- 2 Tbsp olive oil
- 1 lemon, quartered
- 4 garlic cloves, minced
- 2 Tbsp fresh rosemary, chopped
- 2 Tbsp fresh thyme, chopped
- 1 Tbsp fresh parsley, chopped
- Salt and pepper to taste

DIRECTIONS:

1. Preheat oven to 375°F (190°C).
2. Rinse the chicken inside and out, and pat dry with paper towels.
3. Rub the chicken with olive oil, and season with salt and pepper.
4. Stuff the cavity with lemon quarters.
5. In a small bowl, combine garlic, rosemary, thyme, and parsley.
6. Rub the herb mixture over the chicken, making sure to get under the skin.
7. Place the chicken on a roasting pan and roast for 1 hr 20 min, or until the internal temperature reaches 165°F (75°C).
8. Let the chicken rest for 10-15 min before carving.

TIPS:

- Use kitchen twine to tie the legs together for even cooking.
- Add root vegetables to the roasting pan for a complete meal.

NUTRITIONAL VALUES: Calories: 400, Fat: 25g, Carbs: 1g, Protein: 40g, Sugar: 0g

CHICKEN CACCIATORE

PREPARATION TIME: 15 min
COOKING TIME: 45 min
MODE OF COOKING: Stovetop
SERVINGS: 4
INGREDIENTS:

- 4 chicken thighs, skinless
- 2 Tbsp olive oil
- 1 onion, chopped
- 2 garlic cloves, minced
- 1 red bell pepper, sliced
- 1 yellow bell pepper, sliced
- 1 can (14.5 oz) diced tomatoes
- 1/2 cup dry white wine
- 1/2 cup chicken broth
- 1 tsp dried oregano
- 1 tsp dried basil
- 1/4 cup fresh parsley, chopped
- Salt and pepper to taste

DIRECTIONS:

1. Heat olive oil in a large skillet over medium-high heat.
2. Season chicken thighs with salt and pepper and brown on both sides, about 5 minutes per side. Remove from skillet and set aside.
3. Add onion and garlic to the skillet, sauté until softened.
4. Add bell peppers and cook for another 5 minutes.
5. Stir in diced tomatoes, white wine, chicken broth, oregano, and basil.
6. Return chicken thighs to the skillet, cover, and simmer for 30 minutes until chicken is cooked through.
7. Garnish with fresh parsley and serve.

TIPS:

- Serve with cauliflower rice or zucchini noodles for a low-carb option.
- Add mushrooms for extra flavor.

NUTRITIONAL VALUES: Calories: 320, Fat: 16g, Carbs: 10g, Protein: 30g, Sugar: 5g

LEMON GARLIC CHICKEN

PREPARATION TIME: 10 min
COOKING TIME: 25 min
MODE OF COOKING: Stovetop
SERVINGS: 4
INGREDIENTS:

- 4 boneless, skinless chicken breasts
- 2 Tbsp olive oil
- 4 garlic cloves, minced
- 1/4 cup chicken broth
- 1/4 cup fresh lemon juice
- 1 Tbsp lemon zest
- 2 Tbsp fresh parsley, chopped
- Salt and pepper to taste

DIRECTIONS:

1. Heat olive oil in a large skillet over medium-high heat.
2. Season chicken breasts with salt and pepper and cook for 5-6 minutes on each side, until golden brown and cooked through. Remove from skillet and set aside.
3. Add garlic to the skillet and sauté for 1 minute.
4. Stir in chicken broth, lemon juice, and lemon zest. Bring to a simmer.
5. Return chicken breasts to the skillet and cook for another 2-3 minutes, until heated through.
6. Garnish with fresh parsley and serve.

TIPS:

- Serve with steamed vegetables or a fresh green salad.
- Add a pinch of red pepper flakes for a spicy kick.

NUTRITIONAL VALUES: Calories: 220, Fat: 10g, Carbs: 2g, Protein: 28g, Sugar: 0g

CLASSIC CHICKEN MARSALA

PREPARATION TIME: 10 min
COOKING TIME: 25 min
MODE OF COOKING: Stovetop
SERVINGS: 4
INGREDIENTS:

- 4 boneless, skinless chicken breasts
- 1/4 cup almond flour
- 2 Tbsp olive oil
- 1/2 cup Marsala wine
- 1/2 cup chicken broth
- 1 cup mushrooms, sliced
- 2 garlic cloves, minced
- 1/4 cup fresh parsley, chopped
- Salt and pepper to taste

DIRECTIONS:

1. Lightly coat chicken breasts with almond flour and season with salt and pepper.
2. Heat olive oil in a large skillet over medium-high heat.
3. Cook chicken breasts for 5-6 minutes on each side until golden brown and cooked through. Remove from skillet and set aside.
4. Add mushrooms and garlic to the skillet, sauté until softened.
5. Stir in Marsala wine and chicken broth, and bring to a simmer.
6. Return chicken breasts to the skillet and cook for another 2-3 minutes, until heated through.
7. Garnish with fresh parsley and serve.

TIPS:

- Serve with steamed green beans or cauliflower mash.
- Add a splash of heavy cream for a richer sauce.

NUTRITIONAL VALUES: Calories: 260, Fat: 12g, Carbs: 5g, Protein: 32g, Sugar: 1g

CHICKEN PICCATA

PREPARATION TIME: 10 min
COOKING TIME: 20 min
MODE OF COOKING: Stovetop
SERVINGS: 4
INGREDIENTS:

- 4 boneless, skinless chicken breasts
- 1/4 cup almond flour
- 2 Tbsp olive oil
- 1/4 cup fresh lemon juice
- 1/4 cup chicken broth
- 2 Tbsp capers, drained
- 1 Tbsp unsalted butter
- 2 Tbsp fresh parsley, chopped
- Salt and pepper to taste

DIRECTIONS:

1. Lightly coat chicken breasts with almond flour and season with salt and pepper.
2. Heat olive oil in a large skillet over medium-high heat.
3. Cook chicken breasts for 5-6 minutes on each side until golden brown and cooked through. Remove from skillet and set aside.
4. Add lemon juice, chicken broth, and capers to the skillet. Bring to a simmer.
5. Stir in butter until melted and well combined.
6. Return chicken breasts to the skillet and cook for another 2-3 minutes, until heated through.
7. Garnish with fresh parsley and serve.

TIPS:

- Serve with sautéed spinach or a side salad.
- Add a splash of white wine for extra flavor.

NUTRITIONAL VALUES: Calories: 250, Fat: 12g, Carbs: 4g, Protein: 30g, Sugar: 0g

CHICKEN AND VEGETABLE STIR-FRY

PREPARATION TIME: 15 min
COOKING TIME: 15 min
MODE OF COOKING: Stovetop
SERVINGS: 4
INGREDIENTS:

- 4 boneless, skinless chicken breasts, sliced into strips
- 2 Tbsp coconut oil
- 1 red bell pepper, sliced
- 1 yellow bell pepper, sliced
- 1 cup broccoli florets
- 1 cup snap peas
- 2 garlic cloves, minced
- 1/4 cup soy sauce or tamari
- 1 Tbsp fresh ginger, grated
- 2 Tbsp fresh cilantro, chopped
- Salt and pepper to taste

DIRECTIONS:

1. Heat coconut oil in a large skillet or wok over medium-high heat.
2. Add garlic and ginger, sauté for 1-2 minutes until fragrant.
3. Add chicken strips and cook for 5-6 minutes until cooked through.
4. Add bell peppers, broccoli, and snap peas, stir-fry for another 5-7 minutes until vegetables are tender-crisp.
5. Stir in soy sauce and cook for another 2-3 minutes.
6. Season with salt and pepper to taste, and garnish with fresh cilantro.
7. Serve immediately.

TIPS:

- Serve over cauliflower rice or zucchini noodles for a low-carb option.
- Add a pinch of red pepper flakes for extra heat.

NUTRITIONAL VALUES: Calories: 280, Fat: 12g, Carbs: 8g, Protein: 34g, Sugar: 3g

EXPLORING TURKEY DISHES BEYOND THE FESTIVE SEASON

TURKEY AND SPINACH STUFFED PEPPERS

PREPARATION TIME: 15 min
COOKING TIME: 30 min
MODE OF COOKING: Baking
SERVINGS: 4
INGREDIENTS:

- 4 large bell peppers, tops cut off and seeds removed
- 1 lb ground turkey
- 1 Tbsp olive oil
- 1 onion, chopped
- 2 garlic cloves, minced
- 2 cups fresh spinach, chopped
- 1/2 cup grated Parmesan cheese
- 1 cup diced tomatoes
- 1 tsp dried oregano
- 1 tsp dried basil
- Salt and pepper to taste

DIRECTIONS:

1. Preheat oven to 375°F (190°C).
2. In a large skillet, heat olive oil over medium heat. Add onion and garlic, sauté until softened.
3. Add ground turkey and cook until browned.
4. Stir in spinach, diced tomatoes, oregano, basil, salt, and pepper. Cook for another 5 minutes.
5. Remove from heat and mix in Parmesan cheese.
6. Stuff the bell peppers with the turkey mixture and place them in a baking dish.
7. Bake for 30 minutes, or until the peppers are tender.
8. Serve hot.

TIPS:

- Use a variety of colored bell peppers for a visually appealing dish.
- Add some red pepper flakes for a spicy kick.

NUTRITIONAL VALUES: Calories: 300, Fat: 12g, Carbs: 14g, Protein: 32g, Sugar: 5g

TURKEY MEATBALLS IN TOMATO SAUCE

PREPARATION TIME: 20 min
COOKING TIME: 30 min
MODE OF COOKING: Stovetop
SERVINGS: 4
INGREDIENTS:

- 1 lb ground turkey
- 1/4 cup almond flour
- 1 egg, beaten
- 1/4 cup Parmesan cheese, grated
- 2 garlic cloves, minced
- 1 tsp dried oregano
- 1 tsp dried basil
- Salt and pepper to taste
- 2 Tbsp olive oil
- 1 can (14.5 oz) diced tomatoes
- 1/2 cup tomato sauce
- 1/4 cup fresh basil, chopped

DIRECTIONS:

1. In a large bowl, combine ground turkey, almond flour, egg, Parmesan cheese, garlic, oregano, basil, salt, and pepper. Mix well and form into meatballs.
2. Heat olive oil in a large skillet over medium heat. Add meatballs and cook until browned on all sides.
3. Add diced tomatoes and tomato sauce to the skillet. Cover and simmer for 20 minutes.
4. Stir in fresh basil before serving.

TIPS:

- Serve over zucchini noodles or cauliflower rice for a low-carb meal.
- Freeze extra meatballs for a quick meal later.

NUTRITIONAL VALUES: Calories: 320, Fat: 18g, Carbs: 10g, Protein: 30g, Sugar: 5g

TURKEY AND ZUCCHINI SKILLET

PREPARATION TIME: 10 min
COOKING TIME: 20 min
MODE OF COOKING: Stovetop
SERVINGS: 4
INGREDIENTS:

- 1 lb ground turkey
- 2 Tbsp olive oil
- 1 onion, chopped
- 2 garlic cloves, minced
- 2 zucchinis, sliced
- 1 red bell pepper, chopped
- 1 tsp dried thyme
- 1 tsp dried rosemary
- Salt and pepper to taste

DIRECTIONS:

1. Heat olive oil in a large skillet over medium heat. Add onion and garlic, sauté until softened.
2. Add ground turkey and cook until browned.
3. Stir in zucchini, bell pepper, thyme, rosemary, salt, and pepper.
4. Cook for another 10 minutes, or until the vegetables are tender.

5. Serve hot.

TIPS:

- Top with a sprinkle of Parmesan cheese for added flavor.
- Add some cherry tomatoes for extra color and taste.

NUTRITIONAL VALUES: Calories: 280, Fat: 14g, Carbs: 8g, Protein: 30g, Sugar: 4g

TURKEY LETTUCE WRAPS

PREPARATION TIME: 15 min
COOKING TIME: 10 min
MODE OF COOKING: Stovetop
SERVINGS: 4
INGREDIENTS:

- 1 lb ground turkey
- 1 Tbsp olive oil
- 1 onion, chopped
- 2 garlic cloves, minced
- 1/4 cup hoisin sauce
- 2 Tbsp soy sauce or tamari
- 1 Tbsp rice vinegar
- 1 tsp fresh ginger, grated
- 1 head butter lettuce, leaves separated
- 1/4 cup chopped green onions
- 1/4 cup shredded carrots

DIRECTIONS:

1. Heat olive oil in a large skillet over medium heat. Add onion and garlic, sauté until softened.
2. Add ground turkey and cook until browned.
3. Stir in hoisin sauce, soy sauce, rice vinegar, and ginger. Cook for another 2-3 minutes.
4. Spoon the turkey mixture into lettuce leaves and top with green onions and shredded carrots.
5. Serve immediately.

TIPS:

- Add chopped water chestnuts for extra crunch.
- Serve with a side of cauliflower rice for a complete meal.

NUTRITIONAL VALUES: Calories: 240, Fat: 10g, Carbs: 12g, Protein: 26g, Sugar: 6g

TURKEY AND VEGETABLE STIR-FRY

PREPARATION TIME: 15 min
COOKING TIME: 15 min
MODE OF COOKING: Stovetop
SERVINGS: 4
INGREDIENTS:

- 1 lb turkey breast, sliced into strips
- 2 Tbsp coconut oil
- 1 onion, sliced
- 2 garlic cloves, minced
- 1 red bell pepper, sliced
- 1 yellow bell pepper, sliced
- 1 cup broccoli florets
- 1 cup snap peas
- 1/4 cup soy sauce or tamari
- 1 Tbsp fresh ginger, grated
- 2 Tbsp fresh cilantro, chopped
- Salt and pepper to taste

DIRECTIONS:

1. Heat coconut oil in a large skillet or wok over medium-high heat.
2. Add onion and garlic, sauté for 1-2 minutes until fragrant.

3. Add turkey strips and cook for 5-6 minutes until cooked through.
4. Add bell peppers, broccoli, and snap peas, stir-fry for another 5-7 minutes until vegetables are tender-crisp.
5. Stir in soy sauce and ginger, cook for another 2-3 minutes.
6. Season with salt and pepper to taste, and garnish with fresh cilantro.
7. Serve immediately.

TIPS:

- Serve over cauliflower rice or zucchini noodles for a low-carb option.
- Add a pinch of red pepper flakes for extra heat.

NUTRITIONAL VALUES: Calories: 290, Fat: 12g, Carbs: 10g, Protein: 36g, Sugar: 4g

TURKEY CHILI

PREPARATION TIME: 10 min
COOKING TIME: 40 min
MODE OF COOKING: Stovetop
SERVINGS: 6
INGREDIENTS:

- 1 lb ground turkey
- 1 Tbsp olive oil
- 1 onion, chopped
- 2 garlic cloves, minced
- 1 red bell pepper, chopped
- 1 can (14.5 oz) diced tomatoes
- 1 cup chicken broth
- 1 Tbsp chili powder
- 1 tsp cumin
- 1 tsp paprika
- 1/2 tsp cayenne pepper (optional)
- 1/4 cup fresh cilantro, chopped
- Salt and pepper to taste

DIRECTIONS:

1. Heat olive oil in a large pot over medium heat. Add onion and garlic, sauté until softened.
2. Add ground turkey and cook until browned.
3. Stir in bell pepper, diced tomatoes, chicken broth, chili powder, cumin, paprika, cayenne pepper, salt, and pepper.
4. Bring to a simmer and cook for 30 minutes, stirring occasionally.
5. Stir in fresh cilantro before serving.

TIPS:

- Serve with avocado slices and a dollop of Greek yogurt.
- Add black beans for extra protein and fiber (optional).

NUTRITIONAL VALUES: Calories: 250, Fat: 12g, Carbs: 12g, Protein: 26g, Sugar: 6g

SIMPLE ONE-DISH POULTRY MEALS

CHICKEN AND VEGETABLE SHEET PAN DINNER

PREPARATION TIME: 15 min
COOKING TIME: 30 min
MODE OF COOKING: Baking
SERVINGS: 4
INGREDIENTS:

- 4 boneless, skinless chicken breasts
- 2 cups broccoli florets
- 1 red bell pepper, sliced
- 1 yellow bell pepper, sliced
- 1 zucchini, sliced
- 2 Tbsp olive oil
- 1 tsp garlic powder
- 1 tsp paprika
- 1 tsp dried thyme
- Salt and pepper to taste
- Lemon wedges for serving

DIRECTIONS:

1. Preheat oven to 400°F (200°C).
2. Place chicken breasts and vegetables on a large baking sheet.
3. Drizzle olive oil over the chicken and vegetables.
4. Sprinkle garlic powder, paprika, thyme, salt, and pepper over everything.
5. Toss the vegetables to coat evenly.
6. Bake for 25-30 minutes, or until the chicken is cooked through and the vegetables are tender.
7. Serve with lemon wedges.

TIPS:

- Use parchment paper for easy cleanup.
- Add a sprinkle of Parmesan cheese before serving.

NUTRITIONAL VALUES: Calories: 320, Fat: 12g, Carbs: 10g, Protein: 40g, Sugar: 3g

CHICKEN AND CAULIFLOWER RICE CASSEROLE

PREPARATION TIME: 15 min
COOKING TIME: 30 min
MODE OF COOKING: Baking
SERVINGS: 4
INGREDIENTS:

- 2 cups cauliflower rice
- 2 cups cooked chicken breast, shredded
- 1 cup broccoli florets
- 1/2 cup shredded cheddar cheese
- 1/4 cup grated Parmesan cheese
- 1/2 cup Greek yogurt
- 1/4 cup chicken broth
- 1 tsp garlic powder
- 1 tsp onion powder
- Salt and pepper to taste

DIRECTIONS:

1. Preheat oven to 375°F (190°C).
2. In a large bowl, combine cauliflower rice, shredded chicken, broccoli, cheddar cheese, Parmesan cheese, Greek yogurt, chicken broth, garlic powder, onion powder, salt, and pepper.
3. Mix until well combined.
4. Transfer to a baking dish and spread evenly.
5. Bake for 25-30 minutes, or until the casserole is bubbly and golden brown.
6. Serve hot.

TIPS:

- Use rotisserie chicken for a quicker preparation.
- Add some chopped fresh herbs for extra flavor.

NUTRITIONAL VALUES: Calories: 290, Fat: 15g, Carbs: 8g, Protein: 30g, Sugar: 2g

CHICKEN AND SPINACH SKILLET

PREPARATION TIME: 10 min
COOKING TIME: 20 min
MODE OF COOKING: Stovetop
SERVINGS: 4
INGREDIENTS:

- 4 boneless, skinless chicken breasts
- 2 Tbsp olive oil
- 1 onion, chopped
- 3 garlic cloves, minced
- 4 cups fresh spinach
- 1 cup cherry tomatoes, halved
- 1/4 cup chicken broth
- 1/4 cup grated Parmesan cheese
- Salt and pepper to taste

DIRECTIONS:

1. Heat olive oil in a large skillet over medium-high heat.
2. Season chicken breasts with salt and pepper, then add to the skillet. Cook for 5-6 minutes on each side until golden brown and cooked

through. Remove from the skillet and set aside.

3. In the same skillet, add onion and garlic. Sauté until softened.

4. Add spinach and cherry tomatoes. Cook until the spinach is wilted.

5. Stir in chicken broth and Parmesan cheese. Cook for another 2-3 minutes.

6. Return chicken to the skillet and heat through.

7. Serve hot.

TIPS:

- Use baby spinach for a more tender texture.
- Add a splash of lemon juice for extra brightness.

NUTRITIONAL VALUES: Calories: 280, Fat: 12g, Carbs: 6g, Protein: 36g, Sugar: 2g

---

ONE-PAN CHICKEN AND ASPARAGUS

PREPARATION TIME: 10 min
COOKING TIME: 25 min
MODE OF COOKING: Baking
SERVINGS: 4
INGREDIENTS:

- 4 boneless, skinless chicken thighs
- 1 lb asparagus, trimmed
- 2 Tbsp olive oil
- 1 tsp garlic powder
- 1 tsp dried thyme
- 1 tsp paprika
- 1/2 tsp red pepper flakes
- Salt and pepper to taste
- Lemon wedges for serving

DIRECTIONS:

1. Preheat oven to 400°F (200°C).
2. Place chicken thighs and asparagus on a large baking sheet.
3. Drizzle olive oil over the chicken and asparagus.
4. Sprinkle garlic powder, thyme, paprika, red pepper flakes, salt, and pepper over everything.
5. Toss the asparagus to coat evenly.
6. Bake for 25 minutes, or until the chicken is cooked through and the asparagus is tender.
7. Serve with lemon wedges.

TIPS:

- Use parchment paper for easy cleanup.
- Add cherry tomatoes for a burst of color and flavor.

NUTRITIONAL VALUES: Calories: 290, Fat: 18g, Carbs: 5g, Protein: 28g, Sugar: 2g

---

CHICKEN AND MUSHROOM BAKE

PREPARATION TIME: 15 min
COOKING TIME: 30 min
MODE OF COOKING: Baking
SERVINGS: 4
INGREDIENTS:

- 4 boneless, skinless chicken breasts
- 2 cups mushrooms, sliced
- 1/2 cup mozzarella cheese, shredded
- 1/4 cup grated Parmesan cheese
- 1 cup heavy cream
- 1/2 cup chicken broth
- 2 garlic cloves, minced
- 1 tsp dried thyme
- Salt and pepper to taste

DIRECTIONS:

1. Preheat oven to 375°F (190°C).
2. In a large skillet, cook chicken breasts over medium-high heat until browned on both sides. Remove from the skillet and set aside.
3. In the same skillet, add mushrooms and garlic. Sauté until mushrooms are softened.
4. Stir in heavy cream, chicken broth, thyme, salt, and pepper. Cook for 2-3 minutes.
5. Transfer chicken breasts to a baking dish. Pour the mushroom and cream mixture over the chicken.
6. Sprinkle mozzarella and Parmesan cheese on top.
7. Bake for 25-30 minutes, or until the chicken is cooked through and the cheese is golden and bubbly.
8. Serve hot.

TIPS:

- Use a mix of different mushrooms for added flavor.
- Garnish with fresh parsley before serving.

NUTRITIONAL VALUES: Calories: 350, Fat: 24g, Carbs: 4g, Protein: 30g, Sugar: 1g

PREPARATION TIME: 10 min
COOKING TIME: 20 min
MODE OF COOKING: Stovetop
SERVINGS: 4
INGREDIENTS:

- 4 boneless, skinless chicken breasts, cut into bite-sized pieces
- 2 Tbsp olive oil
- 1 onion, chopped
- 3 garlic cloves, minced
- 4 cups broccoli florets
- 1/2 cup chicken broth
- 1/4 cup soy sauce or tamari
- 1 Tbsp fresh ginger, grated
- 2 Tbsp fresh cilantro, chopped
- Salt and pepper to taste

DIRECTIONS:

1. Heat olive oil in a large pot over medium-high heat.
2. Add onion and garlic, sauté until softened.
3. Add chicken pieces and cook until browned on all sides.
4. Stir in broccoli, chicken broth, soy sauce, and ginger. Bring to a simmer.
5. Cover and cook for 10 minutes, or until the broccoli is tender and the chicken is cooked through.
6. Season with salt and pepper to taste, and garnish with fresh cilantro.
7. Serve hot.

TIPS:

- Serve over cauliflower rice or with a side of steamed vegetables.
- Add a splash of lime juice for extra brightness.

NUTRITIONAL VALUES: Calories: 280, Fat: 12g, Carbs: 6g, Protein: 34g, Sugar: 2g

9. INNOVATIVE SIDE DISHES AND STARTERS

DELICIOUS GRAIN AND BEAN RECIPES

QUINOA AND BLACK BEAN SALAD

PREPARATION TIME: 15 min
COOKING TIME: 15 min
MODE OF COOKING: Stovetop
SERVINGS: 4
INGREDIENTS:

- 1 cup quinoa, rinsed
- 2 cups water
- 1 can (15 oz) black beans, drained and rinsed
- 1 red bell pepper, chopped
- 1 cup cherry tomatoes, halved
- 1/4 cup red onion, finely chopped
- 1/4 cup fresh cilantro, chopped
- 1 avocado, diced
- 1/4 cup fresh lime juice
- 2 Tbsp olive oil
- 1 tsp cumin
- Salt and pepper to taste

DIRECTIONS:

1. In a medium saucepan, bring quinoa and water to a boil. Reduce heat, cover, and simmer for 15 minutes or until water is absorbed. Fluff with a fork and let cool.
2. In a large bowl, combine cooked quinoa, black beans, red bell pepper, cherry tomatoes, red onion, cilantro, and avocado.
3. In a small bowl, whisk together lime juice, olive oil, cumin, salt, and pepper.
4. Pour the dressing over the salad and toss to combine.
5. Serve immediately or refrigerate until ready to serve.

TIPS:

- Add a pinch of red pepper flakes for a spicy kick.
- Serve on a bed of mixed greens for extra nutrients.

NUTRITIONAL VALUES: Calories: 320, Fat: 14g, Carbs: 40g, Protein: 9g, Sugar: 3g

CAULIFLOWER RICE TABBOULEH

PREPARATION TIME: 20 min
COOKING TIME: N/A
MODE OF COOKING: Raw
SERVINGS: 4
INGREDIENTS:

- 1 small head cauliflower, riced
- 1 cup cherry tomatoes, halved
- 1/2 cup cucumber, diced
- 1/4 cup red onion, finely chopped
- 1/4 cup fresh parsley, chopped
- 1/4 cup fresh mint, chopped
- 1/4 cup fresh lemon juice
- 2 Tbsp olive oil
- Salt and pepper to taste

DIRECTIONS:

1. In a large bowl, combine riced cauliflower, cherry tomatoes, cucumber, red onion, parsley, and mint.
2. In a small bowl, whisk together lemon juice, olive oil, salt, and pepper.
3. Pour the dressing over the cauliflower mixture and toss to combine.
4. Serve immediately or refrigerate until ready to serve.

TIPS:

- Use a food processor to rice the cauliflower quickly.
- Add crumbled feta cheese for extra flavor.

NUTRITIONAL VALUES: Calories: 110, Fat: 7g, Carbs: 11g, Protein: 2g, Sugar: 4g

MEDITERRANEAN LENTIL SALAD

PREPARATION TIME: 15 min
COOKING TIME: 20 min
MODE OF COOKING: Stovetop
SERVINGS: 4
INGREDIENTS:

- 1 cup green lentils, rinsed
- 3 cups water
- 1/2 cup cucumber, diced
- 1/2 cup cherry tomatoes, halved
- 1/4 cup red onion, finely chopped
- 1/4 cup Kalamata olives, sliced
- 1/4 cup feta cheese, crumbled
- 1/4 cup fresh parsley, chopped
- 1/4 cup fresh lemon juice
- 2 Tbsp olive oil
- 1 tsp dried oregano
- Salt and pepper to taste

DIRECTIONS:

1. In a medium saucepan, bring lentils and water to a boil. Reduce heat, cover, and simmer for 20 minutes or until lentils are tender. Drain and let cool.
2. In a large bowl, combine cooked lentils, cucumber, cherry tomatoes, red onion, olives, feta cheese, and parsley.
3. In a small bowl, whisk together lemon juice, olive oil, oregano, salt, and pepper.
4. Pour the dressing over the salad and toss to combine.
5. Serve immediately or refrigerate until ready to serve.

TIPS:

- Serve with grilled chicken or fish for a complete meal.
- Add some chopped fresh mint for extra freshness.

NUTRITIONAL VALUES: Calories: 250, Fat: 12g, Carbs: 28g, Protein: 12g, Sugar: 4g

GARLICKY GREEN BEAN AND ALMOND SALAD

PREPARATION TIME: 10 min
COOKING TIME: 10 min
MODE OF COOKING: Stovetop
SERVINGS: 4
INGREDIENTS:

- 1 lb green beans, trimmed
- 2 Tbsp olive oil
- 2 garlic cloves, minced
- 1/4 cup sliced almonds, toasted
- 1 Tbsp lemon juice
- Salt and pepper to taste

DIRECTIONS:

1. In a large pot of boiling salted water, cook green beans for 4-5 minutes until tender-crisp. Drain and transfer to a bowl of ice water to cool. Drain again and set aside.
2. In a large skillet, heat olive oil over medium heat. Add garlic and sauté for 1-2 minutes until fragrant.
3. Add green beans and cook, tossing occasionally, for 3-4 minutes until heated through.
4. Stir in toasted almonds and lemon juice.
5. Season with salt and pepper to taste.
6. Serve immediately.

TIPS:

- Sprinkle with Parmesan cheese before serving.
- Use a mix of green and yellow beans for a colorful presentation.

NUTRITIONAL VALUES: Calories: 140, Fat: 10g, Carbs: 10g, Protein: 4g, Sugar: 3g

FARRO AND CHICKPEA SALAD

PREPARATION TIME: 15 min
COOKING TIME: 30 min
MODE OF COOKING: Stovetop
SERVINGS: 4
INGREDIENTS:

- 1 cup farro, rinsed
- 3 cups water
- 1 can (15 oz) chickpeas, drained and rinsed
- 1/2 cup cucumber, diced
- 1/2 cup cherry tomatoes, halved
- 1/4 cup red onion, finely chopped
- 1/4 cup fresh parsley, chopped
- 1/4 cup fresh lemon juice
- 2 Tbsp olive oil
- 1 tsp ground cumin
- Salt and pepper to taste

DIRECTIONS:

1. In a medium saucepan, bring farro and water to a boil. Reduce heat, cover, and simmer for 30 minutes or until farro is tender. Drain and let

cool.

2. In a large bowl, combine cooked farro, chickpeas, cucumber, cherry tomatoes, red onion, and parsley.
3. In a small bowl, whisk together lemon juice, olive oil, cumin, salt, and pepper.
4. Pour the dressing over the salad and toss to combine.
5. Serve immediately or refrigerate until ready to serve.

TIPS:

- Add crumbled feta cheese for extra flavor.
- Serve over a bed of mixed greens for added nutrients.

NUTRITIONAL VALUES: Calories: 280, Fat: 12g, Carbs: 34g, Protein: 8g, Sugar: 3g

---

WILD RICE AND MUSHROOM PILAF

PREPARATION TIME: 15 min
COOKING TIME: 45 min
MODE OF COOKING: Stovetop
SERVINGS: 4
INGREDIENTS:

- 1 cup wild rice, rinsed
- 3 cups vegetable broth
- 2 Tbsp olive oil
- 1 onion, chopped
- 2 garlic cloves, minced
- 2 cups mushrooms, sliced
- 1/4 cup dried cranberries
- 1/4 cup chopped pecans, toasted
- 1 Tbsp fresh thyme, chopped
- Salt and pepper to taste

DIRECTIONS:

1. In a medium saucepan, bring wild rice and vegetable broth to a boil. Reduce heat, cover, and simmer for 45 minutes or until rice is tender. Drain and set aside.
2. In a large skillet, heat olive oil over medium heat. Add onion and garlic, sauté until softened.
3. Add mushrooms and cook until they release their moisture and become golden brown.
4. Stir in cooked wild rice, dried cranberries, toasted pecans, thyme, salt, and pepper.
5. Cook for another 2-3 minutes until heated through.
6. Serve hot.

TIPS:

- Add a splash of white wine while cooking the mushrooms for extra depth of flavor.
- Use a mix of wild and brown rice for variety.

NUTRITIONAL VALUES: Calories: 320, Fat: 14g, Carbs: 40g, Protein: 7g, Sugar: 6g

Exceptional Vegetable Sides

Garlic Parmesan Roasted Asparagus

PREPARATION TIME: 10 min
COOKING TIME: 15 min
MODE OF COOKING: Roasting
SERVINGS: 4
INGREDIENTS:

- 1 lb asparagus, trimmed
- 2 Tbsp olive oil
- 3 garlic cloves, minced
- 1/4 cup grated Parmesan cheese
- Salt and pepper to taste
- Lemon wedges for serving

DIRECTIONS:

1. Preheat oven to 425°F (220°C).
2. Toss asparagus with olive oil, garlic, salt, and pepper.
3. Spread on a baking sheet and sprinkle with Parmesan cheese.
4. Roast for 12-15 minutes, until tender and slightly crispy.
5. Serve with lemon wedges.

TIPS:

- Add a sprinkle of lemon zest for extra brightness.
- Serve with a poached egg for a complete meal.

NUTRITIONAL VALUES: Calories: 140, Fat: 9g, Carbs: 8g, Protein: 6g, Sugar: 2g

Sautéed Green Beans with Almonds

PREPARATION TIME: 10 min
COOKING TIME: 10 min
MODE OF COOKING: Stovetop
SERVINGS: 4
INGREDIENTS:

- 1 lb green beans, trimmed
- 2 Tbsp olive oil
- 2 garlic cloves, minced
- 1/4 cup sliced almonds, toasted
- Salt and pepper to taste
- 1 Tbsp lemon juice

DIRECTIONS:

1. In a large skillet, heat olive oil over medium heat.
2. Add garlic and sauté for 1-2 minutes until fragrant.
3. Add green beans and cook for 5-7 minutes until tender-crisp.
4. Stir in toasted almonds and lemon juice.
5. Season with salt and pepper to taste and serve immediately.

TIPS:

- Add a pinch of red pepper flakes for some heat.
- Garnish with grated Parmesan cheese.

NUTRITIONAL VALUES: Calories: 130, Fat: 9g, Carbs: 10g, Protein: 4g, Sugar: 3g

Spicy Roasted Cauliflower

PREPARATION TIME: 10 min
COOKING TIME: 25 min
MODE OF COOKING: Roasting
SERVINGS: 4
INGREDIENTS:

- 1 head cauliflower, cut into florets
- 3 Tbsp olive oil
- 1 tsp smoked paprika
- 1/2 tsp cayenne pepper
- Salt and pepper to taste
- 1 Tbsp chopped fresh parsley

DIRECTIONS:

1. Preheat oven to 400°F (200°C).
2. Toss cauliflower florets with olive oil, smoked paprika, cayenne pepper, salt, and pepper.
3. Spread on a baking sheet and roast for 20-25 minutes until golden and crispy.
4. Garnish with fresh parsley before serving.

TIPS:

- Serve with a side of Greek yogurt for dipping.
- Add some grated Parmesan for extra flavor.

NUTRITIONAL VALUES: Calories: 150, Fat: 10g, Carbs: 12g, Protein: 3g, Sugar: 3g

Balsamic Glazed Carrots

PREPARATION TIME: 10 min
COOKING TIME: 25 min
MODE OF COOKING: Roasting

SERVINGS: 4
INGREDIENTS:

- 1 lb carrots, peeled and cut into sticks

- 2 Tbsp olive oil
- Salt and pepper to taste
- 1/4 cup balsamic vinegar
- 1 Tbsp honey
- 1 tsp fresh thyme leaves

DIRECTIONS:

1. Preheat oven to 400°F (200°C).
2. Toss carrots with olive oil, salt, and pepper.
3. Spread on a baking sheet and roast for 20-25 minutes until tender.
4. In a small saucepan, heat balsamic vinegar and honey over medium heat until reduced to a glaze, about 5 minutes.
5. Drizzle the glaze over the roasted carrots and sprinkle with fresh thyme before serving.

TIPS:

- Add a sprinkle of crushed red pepper flakes for some heat.
- Top with toasted sesame seeds for added texture.

NUTRITIONAL VALUES: Calories: 130, Fat: 7g, Carbs: 18g, Protein: 1g, Sugar: 10g

SAUTÉED BRUSSELS SPROUTS WITH BACON

PREPARATION TIME: 10 min
COOKING TIME: 15 min
MODE OF COOKING: Stovetop
SERVINGS: 4
INGREDIENTS:

- 1 lb Brussels sprouts, trimmed and halved
- 4 slices bacon, chopped
- 2 garlic cloves, minced
- Salt and pepper to taste
- 1 Tbsp apple cider vinegar

DIRECTIONS:

1. In a large skillet, cook bacon over medium heat until crispy. Remove and set aside, leaving the bacon fat in the skillet.
2. Add garlic to the skillet and sauté for 1 minute.
3. Add Brussels sprouts and cook for 10-12 minutes, stirring occasionally, until tender and caramelized.
4. Stir in crispy bacon and apple cider vinegar.
5. Season with salt and pepper to taste and serve immediately.

TIPS:

- Add a sprinkle of red pepper flakes for some heat.
- Garnish with chopped fresh parsley.

NUTRITIONAL VALUES: Calories: 180, Fat: 12g, Carbs: 10g, Protein: 6g, Sugar: 3g

EASY STARTERS FOR UNEXPECTED GUESTS

CAPRESE SKEWERS

PREPARATION TIME: 10 min
COOKING TIME: N/A
MODE OF COOKING: No-cook
SERVINGS: 4
INGREDIENTS:

- 1 pint cherry tomatoes
- 1 ball fresh mozzarella, cut into cubes
- 1 bunch fresh basil leaves
- 2 Tbsp balsamic glaze
- Salt and pepper to taste
- Toothpicks or small skewers

DIRECTIONS:

1. On each toothpick or small skewer, thread one cherry tomato, one basil leaf, and one mozzarella cube.
2. Arrange the skewers on a serving platter.
3. Drizzle with balsamic glaze and season with salt and pepper.
4. Serve immediately.

TIPS:

- Use marinated mozzarella for extra flavor.
- Add a piece of prosciutto for a twist.

NUTRITIONAL VALUES: Calories: 80, Fat: 5g, Carbs: 3g, Protein: 4g, Sugar: 1g

AVOCADO DEVILED EGGS

PREPARATION TIME: 10 min
COOKING TIME: 10 min
MODE OF COOKING: Stovetop
SERVINGS: 4
INGREDIENTS:

- 6 large eggs
- 1 ripe avocado
- 1 Tbsp lime juice
- 1 Tbsp mayonnaise
- 1 tsp Dijon mustard
- Salt and pepper to taste
- Paprika for garnish

DIRECTIONS:

1. Place eggs in a saucepan and cover with water. Bring to a boil, then remove from heat and let sit for 10 minutes.
2. Drain and cool eggs under cold running water. Peel the eggs and cut in half lengthwise.
3. Scoop out the yolks and place in a bowl. Add avocado, lime juice, mayonnaise, Dijon mustard, salt, and pepper. Mash until smooth.
4. Spoon or pipe the avocado mixture back into the egg whites.
5. Sprinkle with paprika before serving.

TIPS:

- Garnish with chopped fresh chives for added flavor.
- Use a piping bag for a more professional presentation.

NUTRITIONAL VALUES: Calories: 120, Fat: 10g, Carbs: 3g, Protein: 6g, Sugar: 1g

GREEK CUCUMBER BITES

PREPARATION TIME: 10 min
COOKING TIME: N/A
MODE OF COOKING: No-cook
SERVINGS: 4
INGREDIENTS:

- 1 large cucumber, sliced into rounds
- 1/2 cup hummus
- 1/4 cup crumbled feta cheese
- 1/4 cup chopped Kalamata olives
- 1 Tbsp fresh dill, chopped
- 1 Tbsp olive oil
- Salt and pepper to taste

DIRECTIONS:

1. Arrange cucumber slices on a serving platter.
2. Top each slice with a dollop of hummus.
3. Sprinkle with feta cheese, chopped olives, and fresh dill.
4. Drizzle with olive oil and season with salt and pepper.
5. Serve immediately.

TIPS:

- Use different types of hummus for variety.
- Garnish with a small piece of sun-dried tomato for color.

NUTRITIONAL VALUES: Calories: 90, Fat: 6g, Carbs: 5g, Protein: 3g, Sugar: 2g

SPICY SHRIMP LETTUCE WRAPS

PREPARATION TIME: 15 min
COOKING TIME: 5 min
MODE OF COOKING: Stovetop
SERVINGS: 4
INGREDIENTS:

- 1 lb large shrimp, peeled and deveined
- 2 Tbsp olive oil
- 2 garlic cloves, minced
- 1 tsp chili powder
- 1/2 tsp paprika
- Salt and pepper to taste
- 1 head butter lettuce, leaves separated
- 1/4 cup fresh cilantro, chopped
- Lime wedges for serving

DIRECTIONS:

1. Heat olive oil in a large skillet over medium-high heat.
2. Add garlic and sauté for 1 minute.
3. Add shrimp, chili powder, paprika, salt, and pepper. Cook for 2-3 minutes on each side until shrimp are pink and opaque.
4. Remove from heat.
5. Serve shrimp in lettuce leaves, garnished with fresh cilantro and lime wedges.

TIPS:

- Add a dollop of Greek yogurt for creaminess.
- Use romaine lettuce for a crunchier wrap.

NUTRITIONAL VALUES: Calories: 150, Fat: 7g, Carbs: 2g, Protein: 20g, Sugar: 0g

---

STUFFED MINI BELL PEPPERS

PREPARATION TIME: 10 min
COOKING TIME: 10 min
MODE OF COOKING: Baking
SERVINGS: 4
INGREDIENTS:

- 12 mini bell peppers, halved and seeded
- 1 cup ricotta cheese
- 1/4 cup grated Parmesan cheese
- 1/4 cup fresh basil, chopped
- 1 garlic clove, minced
- Salt and pepper to taste

DIRECTIONS:

1. Preheat oven to 375°F (190°C).
2. In a bowl, mix ricotta cheese, Parmesan cheese, basil, garlic, salt, and pepper.
3. Spoon the cheese mixture into the halved bell peppers.
4. Place stuffed peppers on a baking sheet and bake for 10 minutes until warm and slightly browned.
5. Serve immediately.

TIPS:

- Drizzle with balsamic glaze for extra flavor.
- Use goat cheese instead of ricotta for a tangy twist.

NUTRITIONAL VALUES: Calories: 100, Fat: 6g, Carbs: 5g, Protein: 6g, Sugar: 3g

---

PROSCIUTTO-WRAPPED ASPARAGUS

PREPARATION TIME: 10 min
COOKING TIME: 15 min
MODE OF COOKING: Roasting
SERVINGS: 4
INGREDIENTS:

- 1 bunch asparagus, trimmed
- 12 slices prosciutto
- 2 Tbsp olive oil
- Salt and pepper to taste
- Lemon wedges for serving

DIRECTIONS:

1. Preheat oven to 400°F (200°C).
2. Wrap each asparagus spear with a slice of prosciutto.
3. Place on a baking sheet and drizzle with olive oil.
4. Season with salt and pepper.
5. Roast for 12-15 minutes until asparagus is tender and prosciutto is crispy.
6. Serve with lemon wedges.

TIPS:

- Add a sprinkle of Parmesan cheese before roasting.
- Serve with a garlic aioli for dipping.

NUTRITIONAL VALUES: Calories: 90, Fat: 7g, Carbs: 3g, Protein: 6g, Sugar: 1g

10. COMFORT WITH EVERY SPOONFUL: SOUPS AND STEWS

NUTRITIOUS BROTH-BASED RECIPES

CHICKEN AND VEGETABLE BROTH

PREPARATION TIME: 15 min
COOKING TIME: 45 min
MODE OF COOKING: Stovetop
SERVINGS: 4
INGREDIENTS:

- 2 cups cooked chicken breast, shredded
- 1 Tbsp olive oil
- 1 onion, chopped
- 2 garlic cloves, minced
- 2 carrots, sliced
- 2 celery stalks, sliced
- 1 zucchini, chopped
- 6 cups chicken broth
- 1 tsp dried thyme
- 1 tsp dried oregano
- Salt and pepper to taste
- Fresh parsley, chopped, for garnish

DIRECTIONS:

1. In a large pot, heat olive oil over medium heat. Add onion and garlic, sauté until softened.
2. Add carrots, celery, and zucchini, and cook for 5 minutes.
3. Stir in shredded chicken, chicken broth, thyme, oregano, salt, and pepper. Bring to a boil.
4. Reduce heat and simmer for 30 minutes, until vegetables are tender.
5. Garnish with fresh parsley before serving.

TIPS:

- Add a squeeze of lemon juice for extra brightness.
- Use rotisserie chicken for convenience.

NUTRITIONAL VALUES: Calories: 180, Fat: 5g, Carbs: 12g, Protein: 24g, Sugar: 3g

BEEF AND CABBAGE SOUP

PREPARATION TIME: 15 min
COOKING TIME: 1 hr
MODE OF COOKING: Stovetop
SERVINGS: 4
INGREDIENTS:

- 1 lb lean ground beef
- 1 Tbsp olive oil
- 1 onion, chopped
- 2 garlic cloves, minced
- 4 cups green cabbage, chopped
- 2 carrots, sliced
- 4 cups beef broth
- 1 can (14.5 oz) diced tomatoes
- 1 tsp dried thyme
- 1 tsp dried basil
- Salt and pepper to taste
- Fresh parsley, chopped, for garnish

DIRECTIONS:

1. In a large pot, heat olive oil over medium heat. Add ground beef and cook until browned. Remove and set aside.
2. In the same pot, add onion and garlic, sauté until softened.
3. Add cabbage and carrots, and cook for 5 minutes.
4. Stir in beef broth, diced tomatoes, thyme, basil, salt, and pepper. Bring to a boil.
5. Reduce heat and simmer for 40 minutes, until vegetables are tender.
6. Return cooked beef to the pot and heat through.
7. Garnish with fresh parsley before serving.

TIPS:

- Substitute ground turkey for a lighter option.
- Add a pinch of red pepper flakes for a spicy kick.

NUTRITIONAL VALUES: Calories: 250, Fat: 12g, Carbs: 16g, Protein: 20g, Sugar: 5g

LEMON DILL SALMON SOUP

PREPARATION TIME: 15 min
COOKING TIME: 20 min
MODE OF COOKING: Stovetop
SERVINGS: 4
INGREDIENTS:

- 1 lb salmon fillets, cut into chunks
- 1 Tbsp olive oil
- 1 onion, chopped
- 2 garlic cloves, minced
- 4 cups fish broth or vegetable broth
- 2 cups spinach, chopped
- 1 zucchini, sliced
- 1 lemon, juiced and zested
- 1 tsp dried dill
- Salt and pepper to taste
- Fresh dill, chopped, for garnish

DIRECTIONS:

1. In a large pot, heat olive oil over medium heat. Add onion and garlic, sauté until softened.
2. Add fish broth, spinach, zucchini, lemon juice, lemon zest, and dried dill. Bring to a boil.
3. Reduce heat and simmer for 10 minutes.
4. Add salmon chunks and cook for another 5-7 minutes, until salmon is cooked through.
5. Season with salt and pepper to taste.
6. Garnish with fresh dill before serving.

TIPS:

- Serve with a side of crusty bread (optional).
- Add a pinch of smoked paprika for extra depth.

NUTRITIONAL VALUES: Calories: 220, Fat: 12g, Carbs: 10g, Protein: 20g, Sugar: 3g

HEARTY CHICKEN AND KALE SOUP

PREPARATION TIME: 15 min
COOKING TIME: 35 min
MODE OF COOKING: Stovetop
SERVINGS: 4
INGREDIENTS:

- 2 cups cooked chicken breast, shredded
- 1 Tbsp olive oil
- 1 onion, chopped
- 2 garlic cloves, minced
- 2 carrots, sliced
- 2 celery stalks, sliced
- 1 bunch kale, stems removed and chopped
- 6 cups chicken broth
- 1 tsp dried thyme
- 1 tsp dried rosemary
- Salt and pepper to taste
- Fresh lemon wedges for serving

DIRECTIONS:

1. In a large pot, heat olive oil over medium heat. Add onion and garlic, sauté until softened.
2. Add carrots, celery, and kale, and cook for 5 minutes.
3. Stir in shredded chicken, chicken broth, thyme, rosemary, salt, and pepper. Bring to a boil.
4. Reduce heat and simmer for 30 minutes, until vegetables are tender.
5. Serve with fresh lemon wedges.

TIPS:

- Use bone broth for added nutrients.
- Add a handful of quinoa for extra protein and fiber.

NUTRITIONAL VALUES: Calories: 190, Fat: 5g, Carbs: 12g, Protein: 24g, Sugar: 3g

SPICY VEGETABLE SOUP

PREPARATION TIME: 15 min
COOKING TIME: 30 min
MODE OF COOKING: Stovetop
SERVINGS: 4
INGREDIENTS:

- 1 Tbsp olive oil
- 1 onion, chopped
- 2 garlic cloves, minced
- 2 carrots, sliced
- 2 celery stalks, sliced
- 1 zucchini, chopped
- 4 cups vegetable broth
- 1 can (14.5 oz) diced tomatoes
- 1 tsp ground cumin
- 1/2 tsp cayenne pepper
- 1/4 cup fresh cilantro, chopped
- Salt and pepper to taste
- Lime wedges for serving

DIRECTIONS:

1. In a large pot, heat olive oil over medium heat. Add onion and garlic, sauté until softened.
2. Add carrots, celery, and zucchini, and cook for

5 minutes.

3. Stir in vegetable broth, diced tomatoes, cumin, cayenne pepper, salt, and pepper. Bring to a boil.
4. Reduce heat and simmer for 20 minutes, until vegetables are tender.
5. Garnish with fresh cilantro and serve with lime wedges.

TIPS:
- Add a can of black beans for extra protein.
- Serve with a dollop of Greek yogurt to balance the spice.

NUTRITIONAL VALUES: Calories: 150, Fat: 5g, Carbs: 20g, Protein: 4g, Sugar: 7g

---

GINGER TURMERIC BROTH

PREPARATION TIME: 10 min
COOKING TIME: 20 min
MODE OF COOKING: Stovetop
SERVINGS: 4
INGREDIENTS:
- 1 Tbsp coconut oil
- 1 onion, chopped
- 2 garlic cloves, minced
- 1 Tbsp fresh ginger, grated
- 1 tsp ground turmeric
- 4 cups vegetable broth
- 1 cup coconut milk
- 1 cup sliced mushrooms
- 1 cup chopped kale
- Salt and pepper to taste
- Fresh cilantro, chopped, for garnish

DIRECTIONS:
1. In a large pot, heat coconut oil over medium heat. Add onion, garlic, and ginger, sauté until softened.
2. Stir in turmeric, vegetable broth, and coconut milk. Bring to a boil.
3. Add mushrooms and kale, and cook for 10-15 minutes, until vegetables are tender.
4. Season with salt and pepper to taste.
5. Garnish with fresh cilantro before serving.

TIPS:
- Add a squeeze of lime juice for extra brightness.
- Serve with a side of cauliflower rice.

NUTRITIONAL VALUES: Calories: 180, Fat: 12g, Carbs: 14g, Protein: 4g, Sugar: 4g

CREAMY SOUPS FOR DIFFERENT SEASONS

CREAMY TOMATO BASIL SOUP

PREPARATION TIME: 10 min
COOKING TIME: 30 min
MODE OF COOKING: Stovetop
SERVINGS: 4
INGREDIENTS:
- 2 Tbsp olive oil
- 1 onion, chopped
- 3 garlic cloves, minced
- 2 cans (14.5 oz each) diced tomatoes
- 1 cup chicken or vegetable broth
- 1 cup coconut milk
- 1 tsp dried oregano
- 1 tsp dried basil
- Salt and pepper to taste
- Fresh basil leaves for garnish

DIRECTIONS:
1. In a large pot, heat olive oil over medium heat. Add onion and garlic, sauté until softened.
2. Add diced tomatoes, broth, oregano, and basil. Bring to a boil.
3. Reduce heat and simmer for 20 minutes.
4. Stir in coconut milk and cook for another 5 minutes.
5. Use an immersion blender to blend the soup until smooth.
6. Season with salt and pepper to taste.
7. Garnish with fresh basil leaves before serving.

TIPS:
- Add a pinch of red pepper flakes for a spicy kick.
- Serve with a side of grilled cheese for a classic combo.

NUTRITIONAL VALUES: Calories: 190, Fat: 12g, Carbs: 18g, Protein: 3g, Sugar: 8g

CREAMY BROCCOLI CHEDDAR SOUP

PREPARATION TIME: 10 min
COOKING TIME: 30 min
MODE OF COOKING: Stovetop
SERVINGS: 4
INGREDIENTS:

- 2 Tbsp butter
- 1 onion, chopped
- 2 garlic cloves, minced
- 4 cups broccoli florets
- 2 cups chicken or vegetable broth
- 1 cup heavy cream
- 1 cup shredded cheddar cheese
- Salt and pepper to taste
- Fresh parsley, chopped, for garnish

DIRECTIONS:

1. In a large pot, melt butter over medium heat. Add onion and garlic, sauté until softened.
2. Add broccoli and broth. Bring to a boil.
3. Reduce heat and simmer for 15 minutes, until broccoli is tender.
4. Stir in heavy cream and cheddar cheese, and cook until cheese is melted and soup is heated through.
5. Use an immersion blender to blend the soup until smooth.
6. Season with salt and pepper to taste.
7. Garnish with fresh parsley before serving.

TIPS:

- Add a dash of nutmeg for extra warmth.
- Serve with crusty bread for dipping.

NUTRITIONAL VALUES: Calories: 300, Fat: 25g, Carbs: 10g, Protein: 10g, Sugar: 3g

CREAMY CAULIFLOWER SOUP

PREPARATION TIME: 10 min
COOKING TIME: 25 min
MODE OF COOKING: Stovetop
SERVINGS: 4
INGREDIENTS:

- 2 Tbsp olive oil
- 1 onion, chopped
- 2 garlic cloves, minced
- 1 head cauliflower, chopped
- 4 cups vegetable broth
- 1 cup coconut milk
- 1 tsp ground cumin
- Salt and pepper to taste
- Fresh chives, chopped, for garnish

DIRECTIONS:

1. In a large pot, heat olive oil over medium heat. Add onion and garlic, sauté until softened.
2. Add cauliflower and broth. Bring to a boil.
3. Reduce heat and simmer for 20 minutes, until cauliflower is tender.
4. Stir in coconut milk and cumin, and cook for another 5 minutes.
5. Use an immersion blender to blend the soup until smooth.
6. Season with salt and pepper to taste.
7. Garnish with fresh chives before serving.

TIPS:

- Add a pinch of turmeric for a golden hue.
- Serve with a sprinkle of toasted almonds for crunch.

NUTRITIONAL VALUES: Calories: 180, Fat: 12g, Carbs: 14g, Protein: 4g, Sugar: 4g

CREAMY PUMPKIN SOUP

PREPARATION TIME: 10 min
COOKING TIME: 20 min
MODE OF COOKING: Stovetop
SERVINGS: 4
INGREDIENTS:

- 2 Tbsp olive oil
- 1 onion, chopped
- 2 garlic cloves, minced
- 1 can (15 oz) pumpkin puree
- 4 cups vegetable broth
- 1 cup coconut milk
- 1 tsp ground cinnamon
- 1/2 tsp ground nutmeg
- Salt and pepper to taste
- Pumpkin seeds for garnish

DIRECTIONS:

1. In a large pot, heat olive oil over medium heat. Add onion and garlic, sauté until softened.
2. Add pumpkin puree, broth, cinnamon, and nutmeg. Bring to a boil.
3. Reduce heat and simmer for 15 minutes.
4. Stir in coconut milk and cook for another 5 minutes.
5. Use an immersion blender to blend the soup until smooth.
6. Season with salt and pepper to taste.
7. Garnish with pumpkin seeds before serving.

TIPS:

- Add a dash of cayenne pepper for a spicy kick.
- Serve with a dollop of Greek yogurt for added creaminess.

NUTRITIONAL VALUES: Calories: 210, Fat: 14g, Carbs: 18g, Protein: 4g, Sugar: 6g

CREAMY LEEK AND POTATO SOUP

PREPARATION TIME: 10 min
COOKING TIME: 30 min
MODE OF COOKING: Stovetop
SERVINGS: 4
INGREDIENTS:

- 2 Tbsp butter
- 2 leeks, white and light green parts only, sliced
- 2 garlic cloves, minced
- 4 cups chicken or vegetable broth
- 4 potatoes, peeled and diced
- 1 cup heavy cream
- Salt and pepper to taste
- Fresh chives, chopped, for garnish

DIRECTIONS:

1. In a large pot, melt butter over medium heat. Add leeks and garlic, sauté until softened.
2. Add broth and potatoes. Bring to a boil.
3. Reduce heat and simmer for 20 minutes, until potatoes are tender.
4. Stir in heavy cream and cook for another 5 minutes.
5. Use an immersion blender to blend the soup until smooth.
6. Season with salt and pepper to taste.
7. Garnish with fresh chives before serving.

TIPS:

- Add a splash of white wine for extra depth.
- Serve with a sprinkle of shredded cheese on top.

NUTRITIONAL VALUES: Calories: 290, Fat: 18g, Carbs: 28g, Protein: 5g, Sugar: 4g

CREAMY ZUCCHINI SOUP

PREPARATION TIME: 10 min
COOKING TIME: 20 min
MODE OF COOKING: Stovetop
SERVINGS: 4
INGREDIENTS:

- 2 Tbsp olive oil
- 1 onion, chopped
- 2 garlic cloves, minced
- 4 cups zucchini, chopped
- 4 cups chicken or vegetable broth
- 1 cup heavy cream
- 1 tsp dried thyme
- Salt and pepper to taste
- Fresh dill, chopped, for garnish

DIRECTIONS:

1. In a large pot, heat olive oil over medium heat. Add onion and garlic, sauté until softened.
2. Add zucchini and broth. Bring to a boil.
3. Reduce heat and simmer for 15 minutes, until zucchini is tender.
4. Stir in heavy cream and thyme, and cook for another 5 minutes.
5. Use an immersion blender to blend the soup

until smooth.

6. Season with salt and pepper to taste.
7. Garnish with fresh dill before serving.

TIPS:
- Add a squeeze of lemon juice for brightness.
- Serve with a side of crusty bread.

NUTRITIONAL VALUES: Calories: 220, Fat: 16g, Carbs: 14g, Protein: 5g, Sugar: 6g

COOL SOUPS FOR HOT DAYS

CHILLED CUCUMBER AVOCADO SOUP

PREPARATION TIME: 15 min
COOKING TIME: N/A
MODE OF COOKING: No-cook
SERVINGS: 4
INGREDIENTS:
- 2 large cucumbers, peeled and chopped
- 2 ripe avocados, pitted and peeled
- 1 cup Greek yogurt
- 1/4 cup fresh lime juice
- 1 garlic clove, minced
- 1/4 cup fresh dill, chopped
- 1/4 cup fresh cilantro, chopped
- Salt and pepper to taste
- Chilled water as needed for thinning
- Fresh dill and lime wedges for garnish

DIRECTIONS:
1. In a blender, combine cucumbers, avocados, Greek yogurt, lime juice, garlic, dill, cilantro, salt, and pepper.
2. Blend until smooth, adding chilled water as needed to reach the desired consistency.
3. Taste and adjust seasoning if necessary.
4. Chill in the refrigerator for at least 1 hour before serving.
5. Garnish with fresh dill and lime wedges.

TIPS:
- Serve with a side of chilled shrimp for added protein.
- Add a splash of hot sauce for a spicy kick.

NUTRITIONAL VALUES: Calories: 220, Fat: 16g, Carbs: 16g, Protein: 5g, Sugar: 5g

GAZPACHO

PREPARATION TIME: 20 min
COOKING TIME: N/A
MODE OF COOKING: No-cook
SERVINGS: 4
INGREDIENTS:
- 4 large tomatoes, chopped
- 1 cucumber, peeled and chopped
- 1 red bell pepper, chopped
- 1 small red onion, chopped
- 2 garlic cloves, minced
- 3 cups tomato juice
- 1/4 cup red wine vinegar
- 1/4 cup olive oil
- Salt and pepper to taste
- Fresh basil leaves for garnish

DIRECTIONS:
1. In a blender, combine tomatoes, cucumber, bell pepper, onion, garlic, and tomato juice.
2. Blend until smooth.
3. Stir in red wine vinegar and olive oil.
4. Season with salt and pepper to taste.
5. Chill in the refrigerator for at least 2 hours before serving.
6. Garnish with fresh basil leaves.

TIPS:
- Add croutons for a crunchy texture.
- Use a mix of colorful heirloom tomatoes for added visual appeal.

NUTRITIONAL VALUES: Calories: 180, Fat: 12g, Carbs: 16g, Protein: 2g, Sugar: 10g

CHILLED AVOCADO AND PEA SOUP

PREPARATION TIME: 10 min
COOKING TIME: 5 min (for peas)
MODE OF COOKING: Stovetop (for peas)
SERVINGS: 4
INGREDIENTS:

- 2 ripe avocados, pitted and peeled
- 2 cups frozen peas, blanched and cooled
- 2 cups vegetable broth, chilled
- 1/2 cup Greek yogurt
- 1/4 cup fresh mint, chopped
- 1/4 cup fresh lemon juice
- Salt and pepper to taste
- Fresh mint leaves for garnish

DIRECTIONS:

1. Blanch the peas in boiling water for 2-3 minutes, then transfer to an ice bath to cool. Drain.
2. In a blender, combine avocados, blanched peas, vegetable broth, Greek yogurt, mint, lemon juice, salt, and pepper.
3. Blend until smooth.
4. Chill in the refrigerator for at least 1 hour before serving.
5. Garnish with fresh mint leaves.

TIPS:

- Add a sprinkle of red pepper flakes for a bit of heat.
- Serve with a slice of toasted whole-grain bread.

NUTRITIONAL VALUES: Calories: 210, Fat: 14g, Carbs: 20g, Protein: 5g, Sugar: 6g

WATERMELON GAZPACHO

PREPARATION TIME: 15 min
COOKING TIME: N/A
MODE OF COOKING: No-cook
SERVINGS: 4
INGREDIENTS:

- 4 cups seedless watermelon, cubed
- 1 cucumber, peeled and chopped
- 1 red bell pepper, chopped
- 1 small red onion, chopped
- 2 garlic cloves, minced
- 1/4 cup fresh lime juice
- 2 Tbsp olive oil
- 1/4 cup fresh cilantro, chopped
- Salt and pepper to taste
- Fresh cilantro leaves for garnish

DIRECTIONS:

1. In a blender, combine watermelon, cucumber, bell pepper, onion, garlic, lime juice, olive oil, and cilantro.
2. Blend until smooth.
3. Season with salt and pepper to taste.
4. Chill in the refrigerator for at least 1 hour before serving.
5. Garnish with fresh cilantro leaves.

TIPS:

- Add a splash of balsamic vinegar for depth of flavor.
- Serve with a side of feta cheese for a savory contrast.

NUTRITIONAL VALUES: Calories: 160, Fat: 8g, Carbs: 21g, Protein: 2g, Sugar: 15g

CHILLED CARROT GINGER SOUP

PREPARATION TIME: 10 min
COOKING TIME: 15 min
MODE OF COOKING: Stovetop
SERVINGS: 4
INGREDIENTS:

- 1 lb carrots, peeled and chopped
- 1 Tbsp olive oil
- 1 onion, chopped
- 2 garlic cloves, minced
- 1 Tbsp fresh ginger, grated
- 4 cups vegetable broth
- 1 cup coconut milk
- Salt and pepper to taste
- Fresh cilantro, chopped, for garnish

DIRECTIONS:

1. In a large pot, heat olive oil over medium heat. Add onion, garlic, and ginger, sauté until softened.
2. Add carrots and vegetable broth. Bring to a boil, then reduce heat and simmer for 15 minutes, until carrots are tender.
3. Allow the mixture to cool slightly, then transfer to a blender and blend until smooth.
4. Stir in coconut milk, and season with salt and pepper.
5. Chill in the refrigerator for at least 2 hours

before serving.

6. Garnish with fresh cilantro.

TIPS:

- Add a splash of orange juice for a citrusy twist.

- Serve with a dollop of Greek yogurt.

NUTRITIONAL VALUES: Calories: 190, Fat: 10g, Carbs: 22g, Protein: 3g, Sugar: 10g

---

COLD AVOCADO AND CUCUMBER SOUP

PREPARATION TIME: 10 min

COOKING TIME: N/A

MODE OF COOKING: No-cook

SERVINGS: 4

INGREDIENTS:

- 2 large cucumbers, peeled and chopped
- 2 ripe avocados, pitted and peeled
- 1 cup Greek yogurt
- 1/4 cup fresh lime juice
- 1 garlic clove, minced
- 1/4 cup fresh mint, chopped
- Salt and pepper to taste
- Chilled water as needed for thinning
- Fresh mint leaves for garnish

DIRECTIONS:

1. In a blender, combine cucumbers, avocados, Greek yogurt, lime juice, garlic, mint, salt, and pepper.
2. Blend until smooth, adding chilled water as needed to reach the desired consistency.
3. Taste and adjust seasoning if necessary.
4. Chill in the refrigerator for at least 1 hour before serving.
5. Garnish with fresh mint leaves.

TIPS:

- Add a dash of cayenne pepper for a spicy kick.
- Serve with a side of chilled shrimp for added protein.

NUTRITIONAL VALUES: Calories: 200, Fat: 15g, Carbs: 14g, Protein: 4g, Sugar: 4g

11. ENDING ON A SWEET NOTE: DESSERT RECIPES

ALTERNATIVES FOR HEALTHIER BAKING

ALMOND FLOUR CHOCOLATE CHIP COOKIES

PREPARATION TIME: 10 min
COOKING TIME: 12 min
MODE OF COOKING: Baking
SERVINGS: 12 cookies
INGREDIENTS:

- 2 cups almond flour
- 1/4 cup coconut oil, melted
- 1/4 cup honey or maple syrup
- 1 tsp vanilla extract
- 1/2 tsp baking soda
- 1/4 tsp salt
- 1/2 cup dark chocolate chips

DIRECTIONS:

1. Preheat oven to 350°F (175°C).
2. In a large bowl, mix almond flour, coconut oil, honey, vanilla extract, baking soda, and salt until well combined.
3. Fold in dark chocolate chips.
4. Scoop tablespoons of dough onto a baking sheet lined with parchment paper. Flatten slightly with a spoon.
5. Bake for 10-12 minutes until edges are golden brown.
6. Allow to cool on the baking sheet for a few minutes before transferring to a wire rack to cool completely.

TIPS:

- Add a pinch of sea salt on top for extra flavor.
- Use sugar-free chocolate chips for a lower sugar option.

NUTRITIONAL VALUES: Calories: 150, Fat: 11g, Carbs: 10g, Protein: 3g, Sugar: 6g

COCONUT FLOUR BLUEBERRY MUFFINS

PREPARATION TIME: 10 min
COOKING TIME: 20 min
MODE OF COOKING: Baking
SERVINGS: 12 muffins
INGREDIENTS:

- 1/2 cup coconut flour
- 6 large eggs
- 1/4 cup coconut oil, melted
- 1/4 cup honey or maple syrup
- 1 tsp vanilla extract
- 1/2 tsp baking powder
- 1/4 tsp salt
- 1 cup fresh blueberries

DIRECTIONS:

1. Preheat oven to 350°F (175°C). Line a muffin tin with paper liners.
2. In a large bowl, mix coconut flour, eggs, coconut oil, honey, vanilla extract, baking powder, and salt until well combined.
3. Gently fold in blueberries.
4. Divide the batter evenly among the muffin cups.
5. Bake for 18-20 minutes until a toothpick inserted into the center comes out clean.
6. Allow to cool in the tin for a few minutes before transferring to a wire rack to cool completely.

TIPS:

- Use frozen blueberries if fresh are not available.
- Add a teaspoon of lemon zest for extra flavor.

NUTRITIONAL VALUES: Calories: 120, Fat: 8g, Carbs: 8g, Protein: 4g, Sugar: 6g

AVOCADO BROWNIES

PREPARATION TIME: 10 min
COOKING TIME: 25 min
MODE OF COOKING: Baking
SERVINGS: 12 brownies
INGREDIENTS:

- 1 large avocado, mashed
- 1/2 cup almond butter
- 1/4 cup cocoa powder
- 1/4 cup honey or maple syrup
- 2 large eggs
- 1 tsp vanilla extract
- 1/2 tsp baking soda
- 1/4 tsp salt
- 1/4 cup dark chocolate chips

DIRECTIONS:

1. Preheat oven to 350°F (175°C). Line an 8x8 inch baking pan with parchment paper.
2. In a large bowl, mix mashed avocado, almond

butter, cocoa powder, honey, eggs, vanilla extract, baking soda, and salt until well combined.
3. Fold in dark chocolate chips.
4. Pour the batter into the prepared baking pan and spread evenly.
5. Bake for 20-25 minutes until a toothpick inserted into the center comes out clean.
6. Allow to cool completely in the pan before cutting into squares.

TIPS:
- Add a sprinkle of sea salt on top for a sweet-salty flavor.
- Store in the refrigerator for a fudgier texture.

NUTRITIONAL VALUES: Calories: 140, Fat: 10g, Carbs: 10g, Protein: 4g, Sugar: 6g

ALMOND BUTTER BLONDIES

PREPARATION TIME: 10 min
COOKING TIME: 20 min
MODE OF COOKING: Baking
SERVINGS: 12 blondies
INGREDIENTS:
- 1 cup almond butter
- 1/4 cup honey or maple syrup
- 1/4 cup coconut flour
- 2 large eggs
- 1 tsp vanilla extract
- 1/2 tsp baking soda
- 1/4 tsp salt
- 1/2 cup dark chocolate chips

DIRECTIONS:
1. Preheat oven to 350°F (175°C). Line an 8x8 inch baking pan with parchment paper.
2. In a large bowl, mix almond butter, honey, coconut flour, eggs, vanilla extract, baking soda, and salt until well combined.
3. Fold in dark chocolate chips.
4. Pour the batter into the prepared baking pan and spread evenly.
5. Bake for 18-20 minutes until a toothpick inserted into the center comes out clean.
6. Allow to cool completely in the pan before cutting into squares.

TIPS:
- Add a handful of chopped nuts for extra crunch.
- Serve with a dollop of whipped coconut cream.

NUTRITIONAL VALUES: Calories: 180, Fat: 12g, Carbs: 12g, Protein: 5g, Sugar: 8g

CARROT CAKE ENERGY BITES

PREPARATION TIME: 10 min
COOKING TIME: N/A
MODE OF COOKING: No-cook
SERVINGS: 12 bites
INGREDIENTS:
- 1 cup shredded carrots
- 1 cup rolled oats
- 1/2 cup almond butter
- 1/4 cup honey or maple syrup
- 1/4 cup shredded coconut
- 1/4 cup raisins
- 1 tsp ground cinnamon
- 1/2 tsp ground ginger
- 1/4 tsp salt

DIRECTIONS:
1. In a large bowl, mix shredded carrots, oats, almond butter, honey, coconut, raisins, cinnamon, ginger, and salt until well combined.
2. Roll the mixture into small balls.
3. Place the energy bites on a baking sheet and refrigerate for at least 1 hour to set.
4. Store in an airtight container in the refrigerator.

TIPS:
- Add a scoop of protein powder for an extra protein boost.
- Roll the bites in shredded coconut for extra texture.

NUTRITIONAL VALUES: Calories: 90, Fat: 5g, Carbs: 10g, Protein: 2g, Sugar: 6g

FLOURLESS PEANUT BUTTER COOKIES

PREPARATION TIME: 10 min
COOKING TIME: 12 min
MODE OF COOKING: Baking
SERVINGS: 12 cookies
INGREDIENTS:

- 1 cup peanut butter
- 1/2 cup coconut sugar
- 1 large egg
- 1 tsp vanilla extract
- 1/2 tsp baking soda
- 1/4 tsp salt

DIRECTIONS:

1. Preheat oven to 350°F (175°C). Line a baking sheet with parchment paper.
2. In a large bowl, mix peanut butter, coconut sugar, egg, vanilla extract, baking soda, and salt until well combined.
3. Scoop tablespoons of dough onto the baking sheet. Flatten slightly with a fork in a crisscross pattern.
4. Bake for 10-12 minutes until edges are golden.
5. Allow to cool on the baking sheet for a few minutes before transferring to a wire rack to cool completely.

TIPS:

- Use almond butter for a different flavor.
- Add a handful of dark chocolate chips for a twist.

NUTRITIONAL VALUES: Calories: 130, Fat: 9g, Carbs: 10g, Protein: 4g, Sugar: 7g

DIY FROZEN TREATS

MANGO COCONUT POPSICLES

PREPARATION TIME: 10 min
COOKING TIME: N/A
MODE OF COOKING: Freezing
SERVINGS: 6 popsicles
INGREDIENTS:

- 2 ripe mangoes, peeled and chopped
- 1 cup coconut milk
- 1/4 cup honey or maple syrup
- 1 tsp lime juice

DIRECTIONS:

1. In a blender, combine mangoes, coconut milk, honey, and lime juice.
2. Blend until smooth.
3. Pour the mixture into popsicle molds.
4. Insert sticks and freeze for at least 4 hours, or until solid.
5. To release the popsicles, run warm water over the outside of the molds for a few seconds.

TIPS:

- Add a few fresh mint leaves to the blender for extra freshness.
- Use silicone molds for easy removal.

NUTRITIONAL VALUES: Calories: 110, Fat: 5g, Carbs: 18g, Protein: 1g, Sugar: 15g

STRAWBERRY YOGURT BITES

PREPARATION TIME: 10 min
COOKING TIME: N/A
MODE OF COOKING: Freezing
SERVINGS: 12 bites
INGREDIENTS:

- 1 cup Greek yogurt
- 1 cup fresh strawberries, chopped
- 2 Tbsp honey or maple syrup
- 1 tsp vanilla extract

DIRECTIONS:

1. In a bowl, mix Greek yogurt, honey, and vanilla extract until well combined.
2. Gently fold in chopped strawberries.
3. Spoon the mixture into silicone ice cube trays or mini muffin molds.
4. Freeze for at least 2 hours, or until solid.
5. Pop the bites out of the molds and serve.

TIPS:

- Add a sprinkle of granola on top before freezing for a crunchy texture.
- Use blueberries or raspberries for variety.

NUTRITIONAL VALUES: Calories: 40, Fat: 1g, Carbs: 6g, Protein: 3g, Sugar: 5g

AVOCADO LIME SORBET

PREPARATION TIME: 10 min
COOKING TIME: N/A
MODE OF COOKING: Freezing
SERVINGS: 4
INGREDIENTS:
- 2 ripe avocados
- 1/2 cup fresh lime juice
- 1/4 cup honey or maple syrup
- 1/2 cup coconut milk

DIRECTIONS:
1. In a blender, combine avocados, lime juice, honey, and coconut milk.
2. Blend until smooth.
3. Pour the mixture into a shallow dish and freeze for 2-3 hours, stirring every 30 minutes until smooth and frozen.
4. Scoop and serve.

TIPS:
- Garnish with lime zest for added flavor.
- Use a food processor if the mixture becomes too hard to stir.

NUTRITIONAL VALUES: Calories: 150, Fat: 10g, Carbs: 15g, Protein: 2g, Sugar: 10g

CHOCOLATE BANANA ICE CREAM

PREPARATION TIME: 5 min
COOKING TIME: N/A
MODE OF COOKING: Freezing
SERVINGS: 4
INGREDIENTS:
- 4 ripe bananas, sliced and frozen
- 2 Tbsp cocoa powder
- 1/4 cup almond milk
- 1 tsp vanilla extract

DIRECTIONS:
1. In a food processor, combine frozen banana slices, cocoa powder, almond milk, and vanilla extract.
2. Blend until smooth and creamy, scraping down the sides as needed.
3. Serve immediately as soft-serve or freeze for 1-2 hours for a firmer texture.

TIPS:
- Add a tablespoon of peanut butter for a chocolate-peanut butter flavor.
- Top with chopped nuts or berries for extra texture.

NUTRITIONAL VALUES: Calories: 100, Fat: 1g, Carbs: 25g, Protein: 1g, Sugar: 14g

RASPBERRY COCONUT ICE CREAM

PREPARATION TIME: 10 min
COOKING TIME: N/A
MODE OF COOKING: Freezing
SERVINGS: 4
INGREDIENTS:
- 2 cups frozen raspberries
- 1 cup coconut milk
- 1/4 cup honey or maple syrup
- 1 tsp vanilla extract

DIRECTIONS:
1. In a blender, combine frozen raspberries, coconut milk, honey, and vanilla extract.
2. Blend until smooth.
3. Pour the mixture into a shallow dish and freeze for 2-3 hours, stirring every 30 minutes until smooth and frozen.
4. Scoop and serve.

TIPS:
- Add a squeeze of lemon juice for a tangy twist.
- Use other berries like strawberries or blackberries for variety.

NUTRITIONAL VALUES: Calories: 120, Fat: 5g, Carbs: 19g, Protein: 1g, Sugar: 14g

MATCHA COCONUT POPSICLES

PREPARATION TIME: 10 min
COOKING TIME: N/A
MODE OF COOKING: Freezing
SERVINGS: 6 popsicles

INGREDIENTS:
- 2 cups coconut milk
- 2 Tbsp matcha powder
- 1/4 cup honey or maple syrup
- 1 tsp vanilla extract

DIRECTIONS:

1. In a blender, combine coconut milk, matcha powder, honey, and vanilla extract.
2. Blend until smooth.
3. Pour the mixture into popsicle molds.
4. Insert sticks and freeze for at least 4 hours, or until solid.
5. To release the popsicles, run warm water over the outside of the molds for a few seconds.

TIPS:

- Add a handful of shredded coconut to the mixture for added texture.
- Use silicone molds for easy removal.

NUTRITIONAL VALUES: Calories: 100, Fat: 7g, Carbs: 11g, Protein: 1g, Sugar: 10g

EASY AND NUTRITIOUS SWEETS

ALMOND BUTTER CHOCOLATE ENERGY BALLS

PREPARATION TIME: 10 min
COOKING TIME: N/A
MODE OF COOKING: No-cook
SERVINGS: 12 balls
INGREDIENTS:

- 1 cup almond butter
- 1/4 cup honey or maple syrup
- 1/4 cup cocoa powder
- 1/2 cup rolled oats
- 1/4 cup dark chocolate chips
- 1 tsp vanilla extract
- Pinch of salt

DIRECTIONS:

1. In a large bowl, mix almond butter, honey, cocoa powder, oats, chocolate chips, vanilla extract, and salt until well combined.
2. Roll the mixture into 1-inch balls.
3. Place the energy balls on a baking sheet and refrigerate for at least 1 hour to set.
4. Store in an airtight container in the refrigerator.

TIPS:

- Add a tablespoon of chia seeds for extra fiber.
- Roll the balls in shredded coconut for added texture.

NUTRITIONAL VALUES: Calories: 120, Fat: 8g, Carbs: 10g, Protein: 3g, Sugar: 6g

COCONUT CHIA PUDDING

PREPARATION TIME: 5 min
COOKING TIME: N/A
MODE OF COOKING: No-cook
SERVINGS: 4
INGREDIENTS:

- 1/4 cup chia seeds
- 1 cup coconut milk
- 1/4 cup honey or maple syrup
- 1 tsp vanilla extract
- Fresh berries for topping

DIRECTIONS:

1. In a bowl, mix chia seeds, coconut milk, honey, and vanilla extract.
2. Stir well to combine and let sit for 5 minutes. Stir again to prevent clumping.
3. Cover and refrigerate for at least 4 hours or overnight.
4. Serve with fresh berries on top.

TIPS:

- Add a sprinkle of cinnamon for extra flavor.
- Use almond milk instead of coconut milk for a lighter option.

NUTRITIONAL VALUES: Calories: 150, Fat: 9g, Carbs: 15g, Protein: 3g, Sugar: 10g

BANANA OAT COOKIES

PREPARATION TIME: 10 min
COOKING TIME: 15 min
MODE OF COOKING: Baking
SERVINGS: 12 cookies
INGREDIENTS:

- 2 ripe bananas, mashed
- 1 cup rolled oats
- 1/4 cup almond butter
- 1/4 cup dark chocolate chips
- 1 tsp vanilla extract
- 1/2 tsp cinnamon

DIRECTIONS:

1. Preheat oven to 350°F (175°C). Line a baking sheet with parchment paper.
2. In a large bowl, mix mashed bananas, oats, almond butter, chocolate chips, vanilla extract,

and cinnamon until well combined.

3. Drop tablespoons of dough onto the baking sheet and flatten slightly.
4. Bake for 12-15 minutes until golden brown.
5. Allow to cool on the baking sheet for a few minutes before transferring to a wire rack to cool completely.

TIPS:

- Add a handful of nuts or dried fruit for extra texture.
- Store in an airtight container for up to a week.

NUTRITIONAL VALUES: Calories: 100, Fat: 4g, Carbs: 15g, Protein: 2g, Sugar: 7g

---

APPLE CINNAMON BITES

PREPARATION TIME: 10 min
COOKING TIME: N/A
MODE OF COOKING: No-cook
SERVINGS: 12 bites
INGREDIENTS:

- 1 cup dried apples, chopped
- 1 cup rolled oats
- 1/2 cup almond butter
- 1/4 cup honey or maple syrup
- 1 tsp ground cinnamon

DIRECTIONS:

1. In a large bowl, mix dried apples, oats, almond butter, honey, and cinnamon until well combined.
2. Roll the mixture into 1-inch balls.
3. Place the bites on a baking sheet and refrigerate for at least 1 hour to set.
4. Store in an airtight container in the refrigerator.

TIPS:

- Roll the bites in crushed nuts for extra crunch.
- Use peanut butter instead of almond butter for a different flavor.

NUTRITIONAL VALUES: Calories: 110, Fat: 5g, Carbs: 15g, Protein: 2g, Sugar: 8g

---

DARK CHOCOLATE ALMOND CLUSTERS

PREPARATION TIME: 10 min
COOKING TIME: 10 min
MODE OF COOKING: Stovetop
SERVINGS: 12 clusters
INGREDIENTS:

- 1 cup dark chocolate chips
- 1 cup almonds
- 1/4 cup shredded coconut
- 1/4 tsp sea salt

DIRECTIONS:

1. Melt dark chocolate chips in a double boiler or microwave, stirring until smooth.
2. Stir in almonds and shredded coconut until well coated.
3. Drop spoonfuls of the mixture onto a baking sheet lined with parchment paper.
4. Sprinkle with sea salt.
5. Refrigerate for at least 1 hour until set.
6. Store in an airtight container in the refrigerator.

TIPS:

- Use mixed nuts for variety.
- Add a sprinkle of chili powder for a spicy twist.

NUTRITIONAL VALUES: Calories: 130, Fat: 10g, Carbs: 12g, Protein: 3g, Sugar: 8g

12. PUTTING THE GALVESTON DIET INTO PRACTICE: 45-DAY MEAL PLAN

WEEK 1-2	breakfast	snack	lunch	snack	dinner
Monday	Berry Spinach Smoothie	Nuts and Seeds	Mediterranean Chickpea Salad	Veggie Sticks with Hummus	Herb-Roasted Chicken
Tuesday	Avocado Kale Smoothie Bowl	Apple Slices with Almond Butter	Grilled Chicken and Avocado Salad	Almond Butter Chocolate Energy Balls	Grilled Lemon Herb Salmon
Wednesday	Peanut Butter Banana Smoothie	Greek Yogurt	Kale and Quinoa Salad with Lemon Vinaigrette	Chia Seed Pudding	Baked Herb-Crusted Cod
Thursday	Tropical Green Smoothie Bowl	Mixed Berries	Asian-Inspired Sesame Tuna Salad	Fresh Fruit	Chicken and Vegetable Stir-Fry
Friday	Chocolate Avocado Smoothie	Cucumber Slices with Hummus	Roasted Beet and Goat Cheese Salad	Cottage Cheese with Pineapple	Lemon Garlic Chicken
Saturday	Berry Protein Smoothie	Carrot Sticks with Guacamole	Spinach and Strawberry Salad with Poppy Seed Dressing	Bell Pepper Slices with Hummus	Turkey and Spinach Stuffed Peppers
Sunday	Greek Yogurt Parfait	Almond Butter Energy Balls	Chicken and Avocado Salad	Dark Chocolate Almond Clusters	Chicken and Cauliflower Rice Casserole

WEEK 3-4	breakfast	snack	lunch	snack	dinner
Monday	Cinnamon Apple Quinoa Porridge	Greek Yogurt with Honey and Nuts	Grilled Mahi-Mahi with Mango Salsa	Sliced Avocado with Sea Salt	Chicken Cacciatore
Tuesday	Coconut Chia Seed Porridge	Apple and Cheese Slices	Baked Dijon-Crusted Tilapia	Protein Shake	Classic Chicken Marsala
Wednesday	Almond Butter and Berry Oatmeal	Fresh Fruit Salad	Grilled Swordfish with Herb Butter	Roasted Chickpeas	Chicken Piccata
Thursday	Flaxseed and Blueberry Amaranth Porridge	Celery Sticks with Peanut Butter	Baked Pesto Crusted Halibut	Veggie Chips	Herb-Crusted Chicken
Friday	Pumpkin Spice Quinoa Porridge	Baked Kale Chips	Mediterranean Fish Stew	Almond Butter on Rice Cakes	Turkey Meatballs in Tomato Sauce
Saturday	Vanilla Almond Protein Porridge	Trail Mix	Creamy Seafood Chowder	Frozen Grapes	Turkey and Zucchini Skillet
Sunday	Spinach and Feta Omelette	Berry Smoothie	Spicy Shrimp and Tomato Stew	Pumpkin Seeds	Turkey Lettuce Wraps

WEEK 5-6	breakfast	snack	lunch	snack	dinner
Monday	Protein Pancakes	Cucumber Slices with Guacamole	Asian-Inspired Sesame Tuna Salad	Veggie Chips	Grilled Swordfish with Herb Butter
Tuesday	Spinach and Feta Omelette	Apple and Cheese Slices	Roasted Beet and Goat Cheese Salad	Sliced Avocado with Sea Salt	Chicken and Vegetable Stir-Fry
Wednesday	Cottage Cheese with Nuts and Seeds	Fresh Fruit Salad	Spinach and Strawberry Salad with Poppy Seed Dressing	Protein Shake	Lemon Garlic Chicken
Thursday	Smoked Salmon and Avocado Toast	Celery Sticks with Peanut Butter	Grilled Lemon Herb Salmon	Roasted Chickpeas	Herb-Crusted Chicken
Friday	Turkey and Spinach Breakfast Skillet	Baked Kale Chips	Baked Herb-Crusted Cod	Almond Butter on Rice Cakes	Turkey Meatballs in Tomato Sauce
Saturday	Vanilla Almond Protein Porridge	Trail Mix	Turkey and Zucchini Skillet	Frozen Grapes	Baked Pesto Crusted Halibut
Sunday	Pumpkin Spice Quinoa Porridge	Berry Smoothie	Chicken and Avocado Salad	Pumpkin Seeds	Creamy Seafood Chowder

WEEK 7	breakfast	snack	lunch	snack	dinner
Monday	Berry Spinach Smoothie	Nuts and Seeds	Mediterranean Chickpea Salad	Veggie Sticks with Hummus	Herb-Roasted Chicken
Tuesday	Avocado Kale Smoothie Bowl	Apple Slices with Almond Butter	Grilled Chicken and Avocado Salad	Almond Butter Chocolate Energy Balls	Grilled Lemon Herb Salmon
Wednesday	Peanut Butter Banana Smoothie	Greek Yogurt	Kale and Quinoa Salad with Lemon Vinaigrette	Chia Seed Pudding	Baked Herb-Crusted Cod
Thursday	Tropical Green Smoothie Bowl	Mixed Berries	Asian-Inspired Sesame Tuna Salad	Fresh Fruit	Chicken and Vegetable Stir-Fry
Friday	Chocolate Avocado Smoothie	Cucumber Slices with Hummus	Roasted Beet and Goat Cheese Salad	Cottage Cheese with Pineapple	Lemon Garlic Chicken
Saturday	Berry Protein Smoothie	Carrot Sticks with Guacamole	Spinach and Strawberry Salad with Poppy Seed Dressing	Bell Pepper Slices with Hummus	Turkey and Spinach Stuffed Peppers
Sunday	Greek Yogurt Parfait	Almond Butter Energy Balls	Chicken and Avocado Salad	Dark Chocolate Almond Clusters	Chicken and Cauliflower Rice Casserole

MEASUREMENT CONVERSION TABLE

Measurement Type	US Measure	Equivalent	Conversion Formula
Weight	1 ounce (oz)	28.35 grams (g)	1 oz = 28.35 g
Weight	1 pound (lb)	453.59 grams (g)	1 lb = 453.59 g
Weight	1 pound (lb)	16 ounces (oz)	1 lb = 16 oz
Volume	1 teaspoon (tsp)	4.93 milliliters (ml)	1 tsp = 4.93 ml
Volume	1 tablespoon (tbsp)	14.79 milliliters (ml)	1 tbsp = 14.79 ml
Volume	1 cup	240 milliliters (ml)	1 cup = 240 ml
Volume	1 pint (pt)	473 milliliters (ml)	1 pt = 473 ml
Volume	1 quart (qt)	946 milliliters (ml)	1 qt = 946 ml
Volume	1 gallon (gal)	3.785 liters (l)	1 gal = 3.785 l
Volume	1 fluid ounce (fl oz)	29.57 milliliters (ml)	1 fl oz = 29.57 ml
Volume	1 liter (l)	33.814 fluid ounces (fl oz)	1 l = 33.814 fl oz
Temperature	Fahrenheit (°F)	Celsius (°C)	(°F - 32) / 1.8

13. CONCLUDING THOUGHTS: COMMITTING TO YOUR HEALTH

EVALUATING YOUR DIET SUCCESSES

Reflecting on your journey through the Galveston Diet is an essential part of the process. This reflection allows you to see not only the tangible results of your efforts but also the more subtle, yet significant, changes in your overall well-being. Understanding your progress can be incredibly motivating and help solidify the healthy habits you've developed.

Recognizing Tangible Outcomes

When you embarked on this dietary journey, you likely had specific goals in mind. These may have included weight loss, improved energy levels, reduced menopausal symptoms, or a general sense of well-being. Take a moment to assess these tangible outcomes.

Weight Loss and Body Composition:

Start by looking at the numbers. Did you lose weight? If so, how much? Beyond the scale, consider other measurements such as waist circumference, body fat percentage, and muscle mass. Sometimes, the scale doesn't tell the whole story, especially if you've been gaining muscle while losing fat.

Energy Levels:

Reflect on your daily energy. Are you feeling more vibrant and less fatigued throughout the day? Improved energy is a common benefit of balanced nutrition and proper hydration.

Symptom Relief:

Menopausal symptoms like hot flashes, night sweats, and mood swings can be debilitating. Assess whether these symptoms have lessened in frequency or severity.

Appreciating Subtle Shifts

Beyond the measurable outcomes, the Galveston Diet impacts your health in less obvious but equally important ways.

Mental Clarity and Mood Stability:

Proper nutrition significantly influences brain function. Have you noticed improvements in your mental clarity, focus, or overall mood? Feeling more balanced emotionally can be a sign that your dietary changes are working.

Digestive Health:

Consider how your digestion has changed. Reduced bloating, more regular bowel movements, and overall digestive comfort are signs that your body is responding well to the diet.

Sleep Quality:

Improved sleep is often an unexpected benefit of dietary changes. Reflect on whether you're falling asleep more easily, staying asleep through the night, and waking up feeling rested.

Identifying Challenges and Adjustments

As you review your journey, it's equally important to recognize any challenges you've faced. Every dietary change comes with its own set of hurdles, and identifying these can help you make necessary adjustments.

Cravings and Hunger:

Did you experience persistent cravings or hunger? This could indicate that you need to adjust your macronutrient balance or meal timing.

Meal Preparation and Planning:

Consider the practical aspects of your diet. Was meal preparation manageable, or did it feel overwhelming at times? Finding a sustainable routine is key to long-term success.

Social and Emotional Factors:

Eating habits are deeply intertwined with social interactions and emotions. Reflect on how social situations impacted your diet and whether emotional eating was a challenge.

Celebrating Successes

Celebrating your successes, no matter how small, is crucial for maintaining motivation.

Milestone Achievements:

Identify significant milestones. These could be losing your first 5 pounds, completing a week without sugar cravings, or consistently preparing balanced meals.

Personal Growth:

Acknowledge the personal growth you've experienced. Perhaps you've developed a better understanding of your body's needs, or you've become more mindful about your eating habits.

Building Healthy Habits:

Reflect on the healthy habits you've established. These habits form the foundation of your continued success and overall health improvement.

Setting Future Goals

Evaluating your progress naturally leads to setting new goals. These goals should be realistic, specific, and tailored to your evolving needs.

Short-Term Goals:

Set achievable short-term goals to keep you motivated. These might include trying new recipes, incorporating more physical activity, or further reducing processed foods.

Long-Term Vision:

Think about your long-term vision for your health. This might include maintaining your weight loss, continuing to alleviate menopausal symptoms, or simply feeling your best every day.

Keeping the Momentum

Maintaining the positive changes you've made requires ongoing effort and dedication.

Regular Check-Ins:

Schedule regular check-ins with yourself. These can be weekly or monthly evaluations where you assess your progress, celebrate your successes, and adjust your strategies as needed.

Staying Informed:

Continue to educate yourself about nutrition and health. Staying informed helps you make better choices and stay engaged with your dietary journey.

Support Systems:

Leverage support systems, whether that's friends, family, or a community of like-minded individuals. Sharing your experiences and challenges can provide encouragement and new perspectives.

ADJUSTMENTS NEEDED IN YOUR EATING PLAN

Listening to Your Body

The first step in making any adjustments is to listen to your body. Your body is a powerful communicator, and paying attention to its signals can guide you in refining your eating plan.

Hunger and Satiety:

Assess how well your current eating plan manages your hunger and satiety levels. If you find yourself feeling hungry shortly after meals, it might be time to increase your protein or fiber intake, both of which help keep you fuller for longer. Conversely, if you're feeling overly full or bloated, consider reducing portion sizes or spacing out your meals differently.

Energy Levels:

Your energy levels throughout the day can be a good indicator of how well your diet is working for you. Persistent fatigue or mid-afternoon energy slumps may suggest that you need to adjust your macronutrient balance, such as incorporating more complex carbohydrates for sustained energy.

Digestive Health:

Monitor your digestive health closely. Issues such as bloating, gas, or irregular bowel movements can indicate that certain foods may not be agreeing with you. It might be beneficial to keep a food diary to identify any patterns or specific foods that cause discomfort.

Balancing Macronutrients

The balance of macronutrients—proteins, fats, and carbohydrates—plays a crucial role in your overall health and well-being. Adjusting this balance can help address specific issues you might be facing.

Protein:

If you're finding it difficult to maintain muscle mass or are feeling hungry between meals, you might need to increase your protein intake. Protein is essential for muscle repair and growth, especially important as you age. Incorporate lean sources of protein such as chicken, fish, eggs, and plant-based options like beans and lentils.

Fats:

Healthy fats are vital for hormone production and overall health, particularly during menopause. If you're experiencing dry skin, hair loss, or hormonal imbalances, consider increasing your intake of healthy fats like avocados, nuts, seeds, and olive oil. These fats can also help keep you feeling satiated.

Carbohydrates:

Carbohydrates are your body's primary energy source. If you're feeling sluggish or having difficulty concentrating, you might need to increase your intake of complex carbohydrates such as whole grains, vegetables, and legumes. On the other hand, if you're experiencing weight gain or difficulty losing weight, it might be helpful to reduce your intake of simple carbs and sugars.

Adjusting Meal Timing

When you eat can be just as important as what you eat. Adjusting your meal timing can help improve digestion, energy levels, and overall metabolic health.

Intermittent Fasting:

If you've incorporated intermittent fasting into your routine, you might find that tweaking your fasting and eating windows can make a difference. Some people thrive on a 16:8 schedule (16 hours of fasting followed by an 8-hour eating window), while others might benefit from a 14:10 or even a 12:12 schedule. Experiment with different timings to see what works best for your body.

Meal Frequency:

Consider how often you're eating. While some people do well with three larger meals per day, others might feel better eating smaller, more frequent meals. If you're experiencing energy dips, frequent hunger, or digestive discomfort, adjusting your meal frequency might help.

Incorporating Variety

Eating a wide variety of foods ensures you're getting a broad spectrum of nutrients and can also prevent diet fatigue.

New Foods:

Challenge yourself to incorporate new foods into your diet regularly. This could mean trying different vegetables, experimenting with new protein sources, or using unfamiliar spices and herbs. Variety not only enhances nutritional intake but also keeps meals exciting and enjoyable.

Seasonal Eating:

Eating seasonally can also introduce variety and ensure you're consuming foods at their peak freshness and nutrient density. Seasonal produce often tastes better and can be more affordable.

Addressing Emotional and Social Factors

Eating is not just a physical act; it's deeply connected to our emotions and social interactions. Addressing these aspects can lead to a more balanced and sustainable eating plan.

Emotional Eating:

Reflect on your eating habits to identify if you're using food to cope with stress, boredom, or other emotions. If emotional eating is an issue, consider adopting strategies such as mindfulness, stress management techniques, or seeking support from a therapist or support group.

Social Situations:

Social events and gatherings can pose challenges to sticking with your eating plan. Plan ahead by bringing a dish to share that aligns with your dietary preferences, or eat a small, nutritious snack before heading out to avoid overeating.

Monitoring and Reassessing

Regularly monitoring your progress and reassessing your plan is essential to ensure it continues to meet your needs.

Regular Check-Ins:

Schedule regular check-ins with yourself to evaluate how you're feeling, what's working, and what might need adjustment. This could be a weekly or monthly reflection where you review your goals, celebrate your successes, and plan for any changes needed.

Flexibility:

Remember that flexibility is key. Your body's needs can change over time due to factors like age, activity level, stress, and overall health. Being open to making adjustments as needed will help you maintain long-term success.

TACTICS FOR KEEPING MOTIVATED

Setting Realistic and Achievable Goals

One of the most effective ways to stay motivated is to set realistic and achievable goals. When your goals are clear and attainable, it's easier to stay focused and motivated.

Short-Term Goals:

Start with small, manageable goals that you can achieve in the short term. These might include preparing a healthy meal every day for a week, increasing your daily water intake, or incorporating more vegetables into your meals. Achieving these smaller goals can give you a sense of accomplishment and encourage you to keep going.

Long-Term Vision:

While short-term goals are important, having a long-term vision helps keep you focused on the bigger picture. Think about where you want to be in six months or a year. This could involve reaching a target weight, reducing menopausal symptoms, or feeling more energetic and healthy overall. Keeping this long-term vision in mind can provide a powerful source of motivation.

Tracking Your Progress

Keeping track of your progress is a great way to stay motivated. It allows you to see how far you've come and celebrate your successes along the way.

Food and Activity Journal:

Maintain a journal where you record your meals, snacks, and physical activity. This not only helps you stay accountable but also allows you to identify patterns and make adjustments as needed. You can also note how you're feeling each day, which can help you connect your dietary choices with your overall well-being.

Progress Photos and Measurements:

Sometimes, changes in your body may not be immediately visible on the scale. Taking regular progress photos and measurements can help you see changes in your body composition that you might otherwise overlook.

Milestone Celebrations:

Celebrate your milestones, no matter how small. Whether it's losing a few pounds, completing a week of healthy eating, or simply feeling more energetic, acknowledging these achievements can boost your motivation and confidence.

Staying Educated and Inspired

Knowledge is power, and staying informed about the benefits of the Galveston Diet and healthy living can keep you motivated.

Read Success Stories:

Reading about others who have successfully navigated similar journeys can be incredibly inspiring. Look for success stories from people who have followed the Galveston Diet and achieved their health goals. Their experiences can provide valuable insights and motivate you to stay on track.

Continue Learning:

Keep learning about nutrition, fitness, and wellness. Understanding the science behind your dietary choices can reinforce the importance of what you're doing and help you make informed decisions. Books, reputable websites, and seminars can be excellent resources.

Stay Connected:

Join online communities or local groups where you can share your experiences and learn from others. Being part of a supportive community can provide encouragement, accountability, and motivation.

Overcoming Challenges and Setbacks

Challenges and setbacks are a natural part of any journey. How you respond to them can significantly impact your motivation.

Develop a Positive Mindset:

Adopting a positive mindset is crucial. Instead of viewing setbacks as failures, see them as opportunities to learn and grow. Every challenge you overcome makes you stronger and more resilient.

Plan for Obstacles:

Anticipate potential obstacles and plan how you'll handle them. This might include having healthy snacks on hand to avoid unhealthy choices when you're busy or stressed, or scheduling regular workout times to ensure you stay active.

Practice Self-Compassion:

Be kind to yourself. If you have a day where things don't go as planned, don't dwell on it. Instead, acknowledge it, learn from it, and move on. Self-compassion is vital for long-term success and motivation.

Creating a Supportive Environment

Your environment can significantly influence your motivation and success. Creating a supportive and motivating environment can help you stay on track.

Surround Yourself with Support:

Spend time with people who support your goals and encourage your efforts. This could be family, friends, or even colleagues. Their encouragement can boost your motivation and help you stay committed.

Make Healthy Choices Easy:

Set up your home environment to make healthy choices easier. Keep nutritious foods readily available, and minimize temptations by reducing the presence of unhealthy options. This simple step can make a big difference in your daily choices.

Create a Routine:

Establishing a daily routine that includes time for meal preparation, exercise, and self-care can help you stay consistent and motivated. Routines create structure and make it easier to stick to your goals.

Finding Joy in the Journey

Enjoying the process is key to maintaining motivation. When you find joy in what you're doing, it becomes much easier to stay committed.

Experiment with Recipes:

Try new recipes and experiment with different ingredients. Cooking and preparing healthy meals can be a fun and creative activity. Enjoying delicious, nutritious food is one of the best rewards of the Galveston Diet.

Stay Active:

Find physical activities that you enjoy. Whether it's dancing, hiking, swimming, or yoga, staying active should be something you look forward to. Exercise releases endorphins, which can boost your mood and motivation.

Celebrate Non-Scale Victories:

Focus on the non-scale victories, such as feeling more energetic, sleeping better, or having clearer skin. These improvements in your overall well-being are just as important as the numbers on the scale.

Reflecting on Your Why

Finally, always remember why you started this journey. Your "why" is your deepest motivation, the reason behind your commitment to your health.

Personal Reflection:

Take time to reflect on your reasons for adopting the Galveston Diet. Maybe it's to feel healthier, reduce menopausal symptoms, or live a more vibrant life. Whatever your reasons, keeping them at the forefront of your mind can help you stay focused and motivated.

Visualization:

Visualize your goals and what achieving them will look and feel like. Visualization can be a powerful tool to reinforce your commitment and keep you motivated.

ENDURING ADVICE FOR ONGOING HEALTH ACHIEVEMENT

Health and nutrition science are constantly evolving. Staying informed about the latest research and developments can help you make better decisions for your health.

Stay Updated:

Regularly read reputable sources of health information, such as scientific journals, health magazines, and trusted websites. This will keep you abreast of new findings and trends in nutrition and wellness.

Attend Workshops and Seminars:

Participate in workshops, seminars, and webinars that focus on health, nutrition, and wellness. These can provide valuable insights and practical tips that you can incorporate into your daily life.

Consult Professionals:

Regularly consult with healthcare professionals, nutritionists, and fitness experts. Their personalized advice can help you fine-tune your diet and exercise routines as your needs change.

Prioritize Self-Care

Taking care of your mental and emotional health is just as important as maintaining physical health. A holistic approach to self-care can enhance your overall well-being.

Mindfulness and Meditation:

Incorporate mindfulness practices such as meditation, deep breathing, or yoga into your daily routine. These practices can reduce stress, improve mental clarity, and promote emotional stability.

Adequate Sleep:

Prioritize getting sufficient and quality sleep. Aim for 7-9 hours per night, and establish a consistent sleep schedule. Good sleep hygiene, such as limiting screen time before bed and creating a restful environment, can significantly improve your sleep quality.

Regular Breaks:

Take regular breaks throughout the day to relax and recharge. Whether it's a short walk, a few minutes of stretching, or simply stepping away from your work, these breaks can help reduce stress and improve productivity.

Maintain a Balanced Diet

The principles of the Galveston Diet are designed to support your long-term health. Continuing to follow these guidelines will help you maintain the benefits you've achieved.

Diverse Nutrient Intake:

Ensure your diet includes a wide variety of foods to provide all the essential nutrients your body needs. Include plenty of colorful vegetables, lean proteins, healthy fats, and whole grains.

Hydration:

Stay well-hydrated by drinking plenty of water throughout the day. Proper hydration supports digestion, energy levels, and overall health. Consider carrying a water bottle with you to make it easier to remember to drink water.

Moderation and Balance:

Practice moderation and balance in your diet. It's okay to enjoy treats occasionally, as long as they don't become a regular part of your diet. Strive for a balance that allows you to enjoy your meals without feeling deprived.

Stay Physically Active

Regular physical activity is crucial for maintaining health and preventing chronic diseases. Finding activities you enjoy can make it easier to stay active.

Variety in Exercise:

Incorporate a variety of exercises into your routine, including cardiovascular activities, strength training, flexibility exercises, and balance work. This diversity can help prevent boredom and reduce the risk of injury.

Consistency Over Intensity:

Focus on being consistent with your exercise routine rather than on the intensity of each workout. Regular, moderate exercise is more sustainable and beneficial in the long run than sporadic, intense sessions.

Listen to Your Body:

Pay attention to how your body feels during and after exercise. Avoid pushing yourself too hard and allow time for recovery. Rest days are essential for muscle repair and overall health.

Foster Social Connections

Strong social connections can significantly impact your mental and emotional well-being. Building and maintaining relationships is an important aspect of a healthy lifestyle.

Stay Connected:

Make an effort to stay connected with family and friends. Regular social interactions can provide emotional support, reduce stress, and enhance your sense of belonging.

Join Groups:

Consider joining clubs, groups, or communities that share your interests or health goals. Whether it's a fitness class, a cooking group, or a support network, these connections can provide motivation and encouragement.

Volunteer:

Volunteering can be a rewarding way to connect with others and give back to your community. It can also provide a sense of purpose and fulfillment.

Set Realistic Goals

Setting realistic and achievable goals is key to maintaining motivation and tracking your progress.

Short-Term Goals:

Set short-term goals that are specific, measurable, attainable, relevant, and time-bound (SMART). These could be related to your diet, exercise routine, or other aspects of your health.

Long-Term Vision:

Have a long-term vision for your health and well-being. This vision can help guide your short-term goals and keep you focused on the bigger picture.

Celebrate Achievements:

Celebrate your achievements, no matter how small. Recognizing your progress can boost your confidence and motivate you to keep moving forward.

Adapt and Evolve

As you continue on your health journey, it's important to remain flexible and adapt to changes in your body, lifestyle, and environment.

Listen to Your Body:

Pay attention to how your body responds to different foods, activities, and stressors. Adjust your habits accordingly to ensure they continue to support your health.

Embrace Change:

Be open to change and willing to try new things. Your health needs may evolve over time, and adapting your approach can help you stay on track.

Seek Support:

Don't hesitate to seek support when needed. Whether it's professional guidance, support from loved ones, or finding a community, having support can make a significant difference in your journey.

Made in United States
Orlando, FL
16 September 2024

51549049R00059